WOMAN
DRESSING-GOWN

A Play in Two Acts

by
TED WILLIS

EVANS BROTHERS LIMITED

ISBN 0237 49200 8

Made and printed in Great Britain
by Lewis Reprints Ltd., London and Tonbridge
PRA 4863

46531926

Woman in a Dressing-Gown

This play was first presented in England at the New Theatre, Bromley, on 11th November 1963, and subsequently opened at the Vaudeville Theatre, London, with the following cast:

AMY PRESTON	Brenda Bruce
BRIAN PRESTON	David Hemmings
JIM PRESTON	Roy Purcell
GEORGIE BARLOW	Christine Finn
HILDA	Joy Stewart
WILLIE	Colin Rix
CHRISTINE	Alathea Charlton

The play was directed by SIMON OATES, *with settings by* GLEN EDWARDS

Time: The present

ACT ONE
SCENE 1 .. .. The Prestons' flat in London, Sunday morning
SCENE 2 .. .. Georgie's flat, an hour later
SCENE 3 .. .. The Prestons' flat, that evening

ACT TWO
SCENE 1 .. .. The Prestons' flat, the following morning
SCENE 2 .. .. The Prestons' flat, late afternoon and evening

No reference is intended in this play to any person, alive or dead.

Running time of this play, excluding the interval, is approximately two hours.

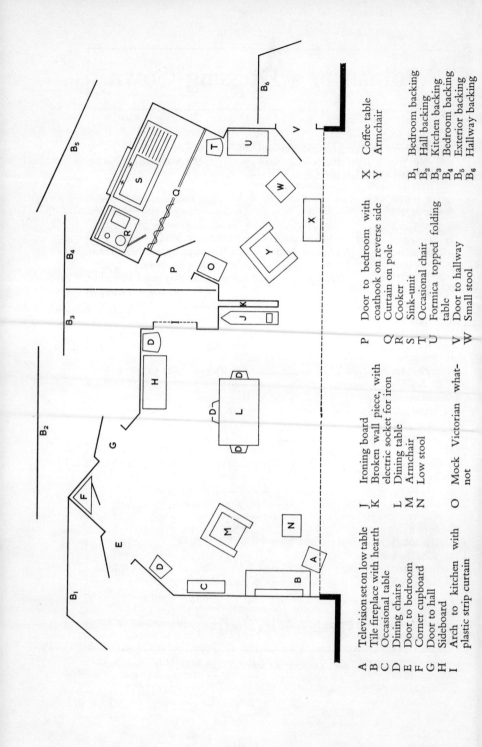

A Television set on low table
B Tile fireplace with hearth
C Occasional table
D Dining chairs
E Door to bedroom
F Corner cupboard
G Door to hall
H Sideboard
I Arch to kitchen with plastic strip curtain
J Ironing board
K Broken wall piece, with electric socket for iron
L Dining table
M Armchair
N Low stool
O Mock Victorian what-not

P Door to bedroom with coathook on reverse side
Q Curtain on pole
R Cooker
S Sink-unit
T Occasional chair
U Formica topped folding table
V Door to hallway
W Small stool
X Coffee table
Y Armchair

B_1 Bedroom backing
B_2 Hall backing
B_3 Kitchen backing
B_4 Bedroom backing
B_5 Exterior backing
B_6 Hallway backing

PRODUCTION NOTE

Woman in a Dressing-Gown is a play about ordinary human beings. There are no villains in it and no great heroic figures. Even the central situation is ordinary, the sort of thing which you can read about in your morning paper. Yet it is none the less tragic for all that; how tragic we can only realize when we are ourselves involved in similar circumstances.

The people in the play are not intellectuals. They cannot rationalize their problems or explain them away. They even find it difficult to talk about them and, at the height of their difficulties, they search desperately for words of explanation, often falling back on clichés. They are decent, kind, average people who are trapped in an emotional crisis which has crept up on them almost unawares and to which there are no hand-made, off-the-peg answers.

It follows that the keynote in any production of the play must be reality. Everything that happens on the stage must appear to be true and real and possible: the audience must be able to identify with the characters. A single jarring note of unreality can disturb the whole balance of the production.

It is important, for example, that Amy should not be made to appear as a slut, for this would destroy the climax of the play. Jim would have no difficulty in making his choice if she were unclean and lazy. She is sloppy, untidy and unorganized, but she is not dirty and her home is not a slum.

In Act One especially both the producer and the actress who plays Amy should avoid any anticipation of the crisis which comes later. Scene 1 and most of Scene 3 should be treated lightly and as much pace and comedy got out of them as possible. They should not be played with any heavy-handed sense of impending doom.

Georgie's flat and, of course, Georgie herself, should appear as a firm contrast to the Preston home and to Amy. But the danger here is to make Georgie seem too cold and almost inhuman. The opening of her first scene with Jim should be light and fast, and again every possible ounce of humour should be got from it. This is almost the only opportunity we have during the play to see Georgie and Jim alone, and it is important also that we should feel them to be very much in love. When Georgie attacks Jim towards the end of the scene, she should be bitter perhaps, but never bitchy. The audience must never feel that she is a designing woman, driving Jim into a situation against his will. She wants him to act for his own sake, because she loves him and believes in him.

Jim is a difficult character to play and, if the actor isn't careful, the character may emerge as a rather unattractive and spineless individual. This would be wrong. He is weak in the sense that he lacks Georgie's self-confidence and certainty of purpose: but his hesitations arise out of a genuine affection for Amy, a desire not to hurt her, and doubts as to Georgie's estimate of his abilities. He is a kind and genuine person who finds it difficult to think only of himself. The actor should seize every opportunity to emphasize the lighter side of Jim's nature. In Act One, Scene 2, especially, we should see him as a man with a good sense of humour, who is attractive to Georgie and who loves her deeply.

In Act Two, Scene 2, where Amy and Hilda get drunk, the players should not overdo the drunkenness. Staggering about the stage and over-slurring of words will ruin the scene and make it distasteful. We should rather see two women on a spree, enjoying themselves. The audience should laugh *with* them, not *at* them. And we should realize from time to time that Amy's thoughts are still on Jim. When she interrupts with a phrase or two from "Oh, Oh, Antonio" this should come in as an echo of the main theme.

Audiences tend to put their own interpretation on the ending of the play and this is how it should be. Some see it as a resolved and happy ending, with the family reunited. Others feel that nothing has been changed and that many problems remain. My only comment is that the producer should not put the answer there for them. At the final curtain we should see a family which has been shaken to its foundations and which still has to work out its salvation, if that be possible.

I have seen this play performed in many countries and several languages and I have never stopped being surprised at its universal appeal. Argentinian, German, Swedish, Dutch and British women have told me that they "know Amy", that a woman like this lives "next door" or "along the road". The few comments I have made here are based on my experience of these varied productions and are an attempt to indicate a few of the possible pitfalls.

What I am sure of, above all, is that it is, in a sense, a simple play, and this is how it should be produced and played—simply, without tricks or melodrama.

I wish you every success with it.

TED WILLIS

*WOMAN IN A DRESSING-GOWN

ACT ONE

SCENE I

The living-room of the PRESTON flat on a Sunday morning in spring. The flat is on the second floor of a block of council apartments, vintage 1955 or thereabouts.

The furniture is cheap but sturdy enough, the room is clean, but the eye-catching feature is its untidiness. Household chores like ironing and mending appear to have been started and abandoned: clothes, papers, magazines, food, have been picked up and put down at random. Thus a teapot and a cup and saucer are on the shelf over the fireplace beside a clock. Two or three postcards have been stuck around the side of the mirror above the shelf R. An old pair of woman's slippers are on the rug C. A kitchen table and chairs are set L.; an armchair in front of fireplace R. Radio on sideboard U.S., against wall above table.

There are three doors. One, U.S., leads to a small entrance hall and to other parts of the flat. Another L. leads to a kitchen, and a third R. to AMY and JIM's bedroom.

The stage is empty. We hear the distant chime of church bells.

After a moment AMY enters from the bedroom. Over a nightdress she is fastening an ancient, stained and shabby dressing-gown. She yawns, rubbing her face with her hands, fighting the pull of sleep. She closes the bedroom door very softly.

AMY is a woman of about 38. Her figure is not what it used to be, and her hair hasn't been blessed by the touch of the professional for years. But with AMY this is not the outward symptom of an internal disorder or depression, or of defeat. She is, in fact, a supremely unde-feated woman, an irrepressible optimist.

She moves R. to the mirror and examines her face carefully. She puts out her tongue, grimaces at what she sees. She tidies her hair a little, looks around for her slippers and finds them on the rug. She slips them on to her bare feet. Humming a snatch of "Clair de Lune", she crosses to the kitchen. She stops, remembering that she hasn't got her normal background of music.

She crosses U.S. to the radio set on the sideboard, switches it on.

There is no response. She thumps the side of the set expertly and is rewarded by a sudden ear-splitting burst of hymn-singing. She turns down the volume hurriedly. She goes to the bedroom door and listens to see if she has disturbed her husband. Satisfied, she crosses towards the kitchen, pausing on the way to take a sweet from a paper bag on the shelf, and pops it into her mouth. A lusty choir is now singing "Onward, Christian Soldiers", and she catches the spirit of it, marching round the room and out to the kitchen in martial style.

Jim Preston *enters from the bedroom.* Jim *is a burly, easygoing, patient man of about 42. He is half-dressed.* Jim *frowns a little at the radio, crosses and turns down the volume lower still. Then he returns into the bedroom.*

A moment later Amy *reappears. She frowns at the radio, crosses and turns it up a little. Then she looks around, as though trying to remember where she left something. She clicks her fingers, purses her lips in an effort to concentrate.*

Amy. Teapot—teapot—teapot— (*She finds it on the shelf. She gets a tray and puts the pot on it, together with some crockery. She lifts a pile of clothes, looks around for somewhere to put them and eventually shoves them on another pile on a chair. A magazine on the floor catches her eye, and she tries to read it as she holds the tray, screwing her head round to do so. She puts the tray down, and picks up the magazine. Pushing away some things on the table to create a space, she starts to read an article. She hunts for and finds a stub of pencil in the pocket of her dressing-gown and begins to work out some figures—reading a little—closing her eyes and murmuring some words—and then marking down a figure. She has found one of those quiz articles which award points for answers to queries.*)

(Brian Preston, *a husky, good-looking seventeen-year-old, comes in from the* u.s. *door. He is wearing a gaudy beachrobe over pyjamas, and has collected the morning paper, which he is glancing at as he enters. He has a slight stutter which is only apparent when he gets excited.*)

Brian. Hey, Mum—how about breakfast?

Amy. In a minute, son—won't be a moment. I'll bring it in to you.

(*He turns and is about to wander back to his room.*)

Brian—listen—

Brian. Mmm?

Amy. It's this quiz. You have to answer these questions, see—

Brian. Eh? Wait. (*He turns off the radio, moves down* c. *to table.*)

Amy. Why did you do that?

Brian. I couldn't hear what you were saying. What did you say?

Amy. It's these questions. This quiz. Now—I want your honest opinion. I want you to be absolutely frank, Brian. Now listen—this is the question—

BRIAN. Tell me what it's about first.

AMY. See for yourself. Here—

(*She hands him the magazine. He reads the headline.*)

BRIAN. "Are You a Civilized Woman?" (*He grins.*) The short answer, Mum, the short answer in your case is no. Definitely no.

AMY (*snatching the magazine with a smile*). Brian, stop it! If I score seventy out of a hundred, I pass. So far I think I'm doing very well. But I'm not sure about number five.

BRIAN. Mum, this is trash. Strictly for the dustbin. You want to prove you're a civilized woman? Right—get some breakfast for your son before he collapses from hunger. (*Sits by table L.*)

AMY. But it says here that the quiz was composed by a panel of eminent psychologists.

BRIAN. So?

AMY. People like that wouldn't sit down and write rubbish, would they? It stands to reason.

BRIAN. Why not? What have the psychologists done to win your respect? You want to know the trouble with the world? I'll tell you. Too many psychiatrists and psychologists. It's an indisputable fact.

AMY (*proudly*). Sometimes—the way you talk, Brian—sometimes you amaze me—you know?

BRIAN (*smiling*). Okay, okay. I know. I talk too much. It's my chief failing.

AMY. No, I didn't mean that. You're intelligent, Brian, you don't want to be ashamed of that. I've always envied people with intelligence. You know my trouble? I haven't got any real opinions of my own. That's the truth.

BRIAN (*with a grin, ruffling her hair*). Who needs opinions? You're fascinating as you are.

AMY (*smiling*). I'll do this later.

BRIAN. That's the stuff—get the breakfast. Dad will be shouting for his tea any minute.

AMY. Your father will be sound asleep. It's Sunday, remember.

BRIAN. He wasn't sound asleep the last time I saw him. He was on his way to the bathroom.

AMY. I don't believe you! I told him to have a lie-in today! (*She crosses to the bedroom door, opens it.*) Jimbo! (*Disappointed.*) Oh, Jimbo!

(JIM *comes to the door. He has washed and shaved, and is tucking his shirt into his trousers. He moves down to fireplace* R.)

Jimbo—I asked you to stay in bed.

JIM. I told you, Amy—I've got to work today. I told you last night.

AMY. I thought you were joking. It's Sunday, Jimbo.

JIM. A new shipment of timber came in from the Baltic. Simpson wants the whole lot checked by morning.

AMY. Simpson! Doesn't he know you have a home—and a wife? Doesn't he think you have a life outside the office?

JIM. Why should he? He lives for the business and he expects his staff to do the same.

AMY. The only difference is that it happens to be his business! Tea ready in a minute. (*Crossing to kitchen.*) Sunday—honestly—Sunday! (*She goes into kitchen.*)

BRIAN. You really got to work today, Dad?

JIM (*with a shrug*). I don't like the idea any more than your mother does.

BRIAN. Dad, why don't you stand up to old man Simpson? I mean, all this Sunday work, this overtime—that's pushing it. You should tell him there's a limit. A man is entitled to some life of his own. Hell, there's a limit.

JIM. I'll get that written up on a big sign and hang it in his office.

> (*They exchange a smile. The relationship between them is a good one.* AMY *enters to collect the tray with the teapot from table.*)

AMY. You'll overdo it—that's what will happen. You'll overdo it, you'll have a breakdown, and I'll be the one who'll have to nurse you!

> (*She goes off with the tray.* BRIAN *crosses to armchair* R., *peers past his father into mirror.*)

BRIAN. You know I'm shaving every day now, Dad? (*He rubs his chin.*) Have to. If I don't shave I look pretty stubbly by five o'clock.

JIM. Who told you that?

BRIAN. Mmm?

JIM (*teasing him*). Christine tell you that? Did she tell you your skin is rough?

BRIAN (*embarrassed, flattered*). Well, you know how it is. Girls sort of notice these things—you know—

JIM. I know. She's a nice girl, Brian. I like her.

BRIAN. At least she's got something between her ears, Dad. I mean—she's got ideas, a point of view; you can discuss things with her.

JIM (*dryly*). She's good-looking, too.

BRIAN (*absently*). Yeh. Yeh—she is quite pretty, I suppose. (*Eagerly.*) Last night, fr'instance, we had a terrific discussion on religion. I've been giving the subject a great deal of serious thought. I shall soon have to make a decision.

JIM. About Christine?

BRIAN. No—no—about religion.

JIM. Oh. In what way?

BRIAN. Well, you see, I happened to tell Christine that I was a Metho-

dist. And she asked me why. I couldn't tell her! Imagine! I've been
calling myself a Methodist for years and I don't know why! It's not
good enough. I mean—here is a fundamental area of belief—and
what do I do? Do I think it out? No. I just put on the family
opinions—as if I was putting on one of your shirts!

JIM. You've been putting on my shirts for the past year. (*With a smile.*)
Not to mention my ties. Which reminds me— (*Calls.*) Amy!
　　　(*He crosses to* R. *of table.* AMY *appears with the tea, and some fruit
juice.*)

AMY (*indicating tea*). It's here, Jimbo.

BRIAN. Dad, I'm serious— (*Crosses towards* JIM.)

JIM (*to* BRIAN). Another time, son. We'll discuss it when I'm not in a
hurry. (*To* AMY.) There's a button off this shirt.

AMY. Did you take it from your wardrobe or from the airing cupboard? All the shirts wanting buttons are in the airing cupboard—
you shouldn't take those. (*She moves* U.C. *of table.*)

JIM (*patiently*). I took it from the wardrobe.

AMY. Did you? How did it get there? Never mind—I'll put a button
on while you're eating your breakfast.

JIM. I don't want anything to eat this morning—just tea.

AMY. You feeling all right, Jimbo?

JIM. I'm fine, Amy! I just don't want any breakfast. All right?

AMY. I suppose so. Only it's unusual. I mean, you always have a
cooked breakfast on Sundays. Are you sure you're all right?

BRIAN. Mum—for Pete's sake! (*Crosses to* L. *of table.*)

AMY (*smiling*). All right. Drink your fruit juice, both of you.

BRIAN. It's rich in Vitamin C.

AMY. It certainly is. And Vitamin C helps to build up your resistance.

BRIAN. Mum, don't you know that a person on a normal diet gets all
the vitamins he needs? It's an indisputable fact.

AMY. Well, isn't fruit juice part of a normal diet?

BRIAN. Yeh—I suppose so.

AMY (*fondly*). You and your indisputable facts!

JIM (*drinking fruit juice*). There! Everybody happy?

BRIAN. I would be if I wasn't so hungry. If I don't eat soon I shall fall
through my trousers and hang myself on my belt. (*Sits in chair at* L.
of table.)

AMY. I'll get your breakfast now. (*Crosses towards kitchen with teapot.*)

JIM. What about this button?

AMY (*turns back*). The button? Oh, the button. I don't know. In this
place a person needs ten pairs of hands. My work-box—where did I
put my work-box? I had it here last night. (*She crosses to fireplace,
puts teapot on mantelpiece and hunts around for work-box.*) Brian! Don't

stand there like one of the seven pillars of wisdom! Help me find it!
Your father's in a hurry.

BRIAN. I wouldn't know where to start.

JIM. Is this it? (*He finds the sewing-box under a pile of clothes on a chair.*)

AMY. Ah. I knew it was somewhere in here. Thank you, dear.

> (*She takes it and crosses U.C. to table. She gets out needle and thread. JIM sits down at the table with a cup of tea.*)

Now, let's see—where's the button?

JIM. Which button?

AMY. The one that came off. Honestly. Where you two would be
without me to look after you, I don't know!

> (*She goes to the fireplace and takes down a tin. She rattles it. It is full of buttons. During this BRIAN gets himself a cup of tea. AMY opens the tin, crosses U.C. to table, and pours the buttons in a cascade on to the table.*)

There should be a shirt button here. (*She scrabbles among the buttons to find one for the shirt.*)

BRIAN. Could I have a bit of the table, do you think?

AMY. Mmm? O, sorry, dear. (*She clears a space by lifting a pile of papers and putting them on chair L. of table.*)

BRIAN. Thanks. Now where do I sit?

AMY. Honestly! I don't know what you think I am, honestly!

BRIAN (*with a grin*). All right, all right.

> (*He drops the papers to the floor and sits down, as AMY selects a button and starts to sew it on JIM's shirt.*)

AMY. While you're out today I've made up my mind to have a real go
at this place. I'm going to tidy it up once and for all.

> (*They exchange a little smile.*)

What's funny in that?

JIM. Nothing. (*She pricks his neck with needle.*) Oh!

BRIAN. I didn't say a word.

AMY. I suppose you don't think I'm capable of being tidy? Anyone
would think to hear you two that I sat down all day and did nothing.
Let me tell you—I'm on my feet twelve and fourteen hours a day
sometimes!

BRIAN. Nobody said you didn't work, Mum.

AMY. Thank you. (*She twists the thread around the button, makes one more stitch and then bites the thread off.*) There.

> (*JIM rises.*)

I'll get your coat, dear. (*She moves out to the entrance hall to get his coat and clothes brush.*)

BRIAN. Do you get paid for all this extra work, Dad?

JIM. Hah! I'm hoping you'll make a fortune and keep me in my old age. (AMY *returns with the coat. She helps him on with it, brushes it down. During this:*)

AMY. They expect too much of you, Jimbo. One of these days I'll go and see Mr. Simpson and tell him a thing or two! Just because he hasn't got a family— You got a clean handkerchief?

JIM (*checking*). Yes.

AMY. I was looking forward to this Sunday. I thought if it was nice we could go out this afternoon—take a ride on the Green Line—a little fresh air would do us both good.

JIM. Look—I'll be home about six. We'll go out then for a couple of hours, eh? I might even buy you a drink.

AMY. Oh, I'd like that. If you're not too tired. I know—I'll ask Hilda and Willie to join us—make a foursome. What do you say?

JIM. Do we have to? I'd like to be on our own. (*There is a slight awkwardness in his manner which she does not sense immediately.*)

AMY. We always ask Hilda and Willie, Jimbo.

JIM (*sharply*). I know, I know. So—just for once, just for a change, I'd like to be on our own. Why must we always have other people around?

AMY. How can you call Hilda and Willie other people? They're our friends. Still—just as you like. We'll go on our own. I'll have some supper ready for you at six, then.

JIM. I shan't want anything to eat. I—I'll get something at that place near the office. (*He moves to the door. He is sorry now that he spoke sharply.*) You can ask Hilda if you want, Amy.

AMY. No. You're absolutely right. We're never on our own these days.

JIM. 'Bye, dear. 'Bye, Brian.

BRIAN. So long, Dad.

(JIM *moves out.*)

AMY (*quickly*). Jimbo!

JIM (*pausing*). Yes?

(*She moves* U.C. *to him and holds up her face to be kissed. He kisses her on the cheek.*)

'Bye, dear. Take care of yourself.

(JIM *goes out.* AMY *goes to the outer door with him and can be heard calling as he clatters down the stairs.*)

AMY. 'Bye, Jimbo! (*She comes back carrying a milk bottle. She crosses* D.R.—*pauses by the mirror, glances at herself. She frowns. She notices a pack of cigarettes on the shelf.*) Jimbo's cigarettes! Your father's forgotten his cigarettes. (*Calls.*)

Jimbo! (*She puts the milk on shelf, picks up the basket and makes a run*
U.C. *for the door. But as she does so the packet opens and the cigarettes
spill to the floor. In exasperation:*) Oh!

BRIAN. You're too late, anyway. Leave 'em—I'll pick them up. (*He
moves across and starts to pick them up.*)

AMY. You know what he is for his cigarettes.

BRIAN. He can buy some more, can't he?

(AMY *crosses to mirror again.*)

AMY (*pulling at a hair*). Imagine that! A grey hair. All of a sudden—
like a visitor. (*Cheerfully.*) Who cares? At my age I should learn to
expect such things. (*She switches on the radio. She thumps it as usual
and twiddles the dial until she gets some music. She picks up a Strauss
waltz. She smiles in pleasure, and, lifting up her arms, starts to waltz
around table* L. *to* R., *finishing* D.S.C.)

BRIAN. Hey!

AMY (*without stopping*). Isn't it beautiful, Brian? I love music. I mean
real music—with melody.

BRIAN. I said—hey!

AMY. I know—I heard you. (*She sings this to the music.*)

BRIAN. What about my breakfast?

AMY (*still singing*). Get it yourself. You're old enough.

(*She waltzes round. He advances on her purposefully. He
switches off the radio in passing, putting cigarettes on radio.*)

BRIAN. That does it!

(*Seeing him coming, she stops dancing, and dodges him. He chases
her round table, trying to corner her.*)

AMY. No, Brian—no—Brian! No!

(*She is enjoying the game, laughing, pretending to be frightened.
He catches her* D.S.R., *and clasping his arms round her, gives her a "bear-
hug".*)

No, Brian—oh—not one of your hugs— No!

BRIAN. Do I get my breakfast?

AMY. Yes—yes—right away. Oh—I can't breathe!

BRIAN (*releasing her*). Okay—

AMY. Oh, Brian—you don't know your own strength! I bet you've
bruised me. (*She picks up knife and cuts off some butter, which we clearly
see on the knife. She goes to the kitchen. We hear a crash offstage from
kitchen.*)

(*Offstage.*) It's all right. Brian—did you think your father looked
tired? (*She comes back to table, still with butter on knife.*)

BRIAN. Yeh. He is a bit frayed around the edges. (*He sits in armchair* R.,
one leg across the arm.)

AMY. He doesn't sleep, you know. I mean—he doesn't sleep properly. I woke up in the middle of the night—he was lying on his back, his eyes open, staring at the ceiling. He needs a holiday.

BRIAN. So let's all pack up and go to the South of France for three months.

AMY (*moving* U.S. *of table*). Wouldn't it be marvellous! I mean—if we had the money—if we could! I've always wanted to travel—Italy, Rome, Florence, Venice—can you see me, sitting back in a gondola, with the gondolier serenading away on a guitar?

BRIAN. They say the canals in Venice are dirty.

AMY. Brian, don't spoil it.

BRIAN. They empty their rubbish into the water—it stands to reason— the canals must be filthy.

AMY. I don't care. One day I shall win thousands of pounds in a quiz or the Pools and we'll all go there. (*She waves the knife up and down to emphasize the point.*)

BRIAN. You'll never win, Mum. People like us don't win.

(AMY *moves* D.S.R. *between armchair and fireplace.*)

AMY. An old widower with only his pension won two hundred thousand pounds last week!

BRIAN. One man in a million.

AMY. It could happen to me! Why not? Is there any reason? One day I shall surprise you. You'll be sitting here with your father, talking as if it were an ordinary, normal day, and I shall walk in with a whole armful of money! And I shall climb right up on that table and scatter it over the pair of you—pound notes and fivers, fluttering down like feathers from a bird, like snow from heaven!

BRIAN. Mum, it's an illusion—a dream.

(AMY *moves to* U.S. *of table.*)

AMY. There's no harm in dreams. Dreams can stimulate a person, Brian. If I won a lot of money—you know what I'd do? First I'd pay for our holiday on the Continent. Then, with what was left, I'd buy tickets—airplane tickets—and send them to people. Anony-mously, of course. Like Mrs. Dekker—she's always wanted to go to Australia—she opens her post one morning and there's a ticket to Australia with a little note pinned to it: "From an Anonymous Well-Wisher"— and the Martins—they've never been able to go to Canada to see their boy—never had the money. Hey presto! One morning—what does the postman bring? Two tickets to Canada! (*She laughs in sheer pleasure at the thought.*) Can you see their faces? Can you see the look on their faces!

BRIAN. Your money wouldn't go very far.

AMY. Far enough. You see—if I won a lot of money and kept it, I'd be afraid it would change our life. I wouldn't want that—I mean—we've got enough—we get along—we're happy. I don't just want to win a big prize so we can live rich—you know what I mean?

BRIAN. Just before you give it away, all that fabulous fortune, remember your son would like a new suit, would you?

AMY. You'll have all the clothes you want! And I'd get your father at least six new suits! (*Seriously.*) You know—I honestly think luck favours some people and not others. Like me, for instance; I've been lucky all my life. Not in money matters—in other things. I've had music playing for me since the day I was born. One day for certain I shall win a really big prize. I honestly believe this, Brian, I honestly do. I feel lucky—know what I mean? (*She laughs, then checks suddenly.*) Oh! (*She puts down the knife on table.*)

BRIAN. Now what's the matter?

AMY. Nothing. Only you shouldn't talk about your luck, they say—that's the surest way to drive it away. (*Thoughtfully.*) Anyway, perhaps I've had my share of good fortune— It's not as if I deserve any more, really. I was thinking this morning when they were singing those hymns on the wireless—I mean, I don't go to church or anything. I never enter a church to pay my respects to God. Oh, Bri—wouldn't it be terrible if I found I'd used up all my luck?

BRIAN. Of all the available mothers, I had to pick a nut like you!

AMY (*dismissing her pessimistic thoughts*). No! It will happen, I know it. I'm confident. One day I'll surprise you—money!—like snow from the ceiling! (*She picks up knife and waltzes out to kitchen.*)

CURTAIN

SCENE 2

The music changes with the scene, switching to the beat of "Lady is a Tramp", with vocal by Frank Sinatra perhaps.

The living-room of GEORGIE'S *flat. It is rather like* GEORGIE—*fresh, neat, cool, feminine, and an obvious contrast to the room in Scene 1. There is nothing expensive about the furnishings. Most of the stuff has been bought cheap and made over with a lick of paint or an attractive cover and the total effect is uncluttered and tasteful.*

There are two doors—one U.S.R. *leads to the bedroom, the other to a small entrance hall,* D.S.L. *The kitchen is incorporated in the living-room—being simply a tiny annexe* U.S., *with sink, racks of dishes, etc., which can be hidden by a trailer-curtain.*

There is a coffee-table D.S.C., *an armchair* R. *of this and a low stool set just above it. A small bureau stands* R. *just below bedroom door.*

JIM *and* GEORGIE *are discovered in an embrace as lights fade in.*

GEORGIE. Love you.

JIM. Love you.

GEORGIE. How long can you stay?

JIM. I've only just got here!

GEORGIE. I like to know. Then I can sort of parcel out the hours—

JIM. I must be home by six.

GEORGIE (*nodding*). Six— I've got some coffee ready.

(*She goes up to the stove for the coffee-pot. She pulls curtain across sink area, comes down to table and starts to pour coffee.* JIM *goes into the bedroom, removing his jacket. Hanging on the bedroom door, clearly visible, is a flimsy robe, belonging to* GEORGIE. JIM *re-enters buttoning on a cardigan. During this:*)

JIM. It's a wonderful day. Really feels like spring at last. Would you like to take a walk across the Heath?

GEORGIE. Would you?

JIM. Not particularly. I'd rather stay here—

GEORGIE. So would I. Unanimous— Besides, I've something rather special to tell you, Mr. Preston. Rather special.

JIM. What's that?

GEORGIE. In a minute, when you're properly relaxed.

(*She lights his cigarette as he settles in the armchair,* D.S.R.)

JIM. What did you do yesterday?

GEORGIE. Thought of you.

JIM. Apart from that.

GEORGIE. Went shopping in the morning. In the afternoon I did some washing and mending. Evening? I went to the local flicks.

JIM. Any good?

GEORGIE. So-so. Not good, not bad. Passed the time.

(*She hands him his coffee. There is a tiny moment of awkwardness, which she covers quickly.*)

(*Sits on stool.*) Have you ever tried a pipe, Preston?

JIM. The way you call me Preston!

GEORGIE. It distinguishes me from all your other girls. Did you ever smoke a pipe?

JIM. Once—years back. Couldn't get on with it.

GEORGIE. Pity. I always wanted to fall in love with a pipe-smoker. You know how it is when you're young—I used to have a very clear picture of my ideal hero—the tough, rugged, pipe-smoking type— you know—

JIM. And you got lumbered with me.

GEORGIE. I got lumbered with you. (*A light kiss.*) You're pretty rugged, come to think of it.

JIM. Thank you.

GEORGIE. Don't let it go to your head. Matter of fact, when I first saw you I wasn't at all impressed. Simpson had been bawling you out, and you looked like you hated the whole world. I thought—murder —have I got to share an office with that!

JIM. Well, if you must know, I felt much the same about you. You were so—so sort of remote, aloof—you know, the type who looks down her nose at the world, as though it isn't good enough for her.

GEORGIE. Did I really give that impression? Really?

JIM. Really—

GEORGIE (*rises*). It's always a bit of an ordeal starting a new job. I suppose I was shy.

JIM. I don't believe that!

GEORGIE. Why not? (*Sharply.*) Don't you think I'm capable of shyness? (*She moves away a little towards* U.S.L.)

JIM. No— I didn't mean— It's just that you always seem as though you have complete control over a situation—you know? Calm, unruffled—

GEORGIE. I suppose I do sort of tighten up when I'm worried or embarrassed— Doesn't mean I don't feel worried. Funny the impression you can give people— I've always thought of myself as being rather weak, as a matter of fact.

JIM. That's definitely not true.

(GEORGIE *moves down to him, smiling.*)

GEORGIE. How did we get on to this? Let's change the subject. I've got some veal for lunch. Do you like roast veal?

JIM. Marvellous.

GEORGIE. I'll put the oven on. (*Moves up, pauses.*) Do you want Yorkshire pudding with the veal?

JIM. Naturally.

GEORGIE. You're a barbarian, you know that? Yorkshire pudding with roast beef—yes—all right. But with veal—ugh.

JIM. It's Sunday. You can't dish up dinner on Sunday without a Yorkshire pudding.

GEORGIE. All right, all right. But one of these Sundays I shall surprise you. I shall make an enormous risotto, or a paella—kebab maybe. Something foreign and exotic. That'll shake you. Yorkshire pudding!

(*She goes behind curtain of kitchen area. He follows her up to* U.S.L.)

JIM. I like that dress.

GEORGIE (*re-appearing from opposite side of curtain* R.). Mmmm?
JIM. I said I like the dress. (*He crosses* R. *to her. He kisses her.*)
GEORGIE (*smiling*). Do you know what I was thinking this morning?
JIM. No?
GEORGIE. Noses.
JIM. What?
GEORGIE. Noses. As I was cleaning my teeth I started thinking about
    noses. You must admit—it's a curious object—a lump stuck in the
    middle of your face with two holes in it.
JIM. You're a nut case, you know that? (*Rubs his nose against hers.*)
    That's what the Eskimos do.
GEORGIE. Why?
JIM. I suppose it's too cold to uncover their lips.
            (*She rubs her nose against his experimentally.*)
GEORGIE. Mmm— No, I prefer our method. (*She takes his arm and
    guides him down to armchair. She sits on the arm.*) You were saying
    about yesterday. I mean—when you come to work it out—what
    did I do? A whole day—twenty-four hours out of my life, and what
    have I got to show for it?
JIM. Some clean laundry.
GEORGIE. No. I mean—there was nothing of real value about the
    entire day. It just sort of slipped over the horizon. Frightens me,
    you know that? I mean—not just yesterday. So many days—they
    come, they go, and they don't leave any sort of mark. Do you ever
    think of things like that, Preston?
JIM. Too often.
GEORGIE. Every day should have some special meaning, shouldn't it?
    Something by which you can remember it. I mean—you can't call
    it back, can you? Frightens me.
JIM. If I added up all the time that has slipped through my fingers—
GEORGIE. I know— (*Thoughtfully.*) Darling—do you know anything
    about Australia? (*She gets up and goes to bureau* R. *and picks up an air-
    mail letter.*)
JIM. Australia—we're hopping about a bit, this morning, aren't we?
GEORGIE. Seriously—this is the something special I warned you about.
JIM. I don't know much. Except that it's big. It has kangaroos, koala
    bears—
GEORGIE. And timber.
JIM. What?
GEORGIE. Timber. Trees—Western Australia has a very important
    timber industry—
JIM (*puzzled, smiling*). What is this? What's all the mystery?
            (*She comes down and sits on stool.*)

GEORGIE. I've got a confession to make. You know I have an uncle in Western Australia—I wrote and told him about us. You didn't mind?

JIM. You told him that—

GEORGIE. I told him that I'd fallen in love with a wonderful man, and that we were going to be married—

JIM. And what did he say?

GEORGIE. He said it was about time. But—and here's the point—I also told him about your job, what you did at Simpsons', your experience in the timber trade—

JIM. Yes?

GEORGIE. Well—read what he has to say about that! Here—this bit—
  (*She hands him the letter, waits happily while he reads it.*)

JIM. A job—

GEORGIE. A good job.

JIM. But he doesn't know me.

GEORGIE. He knows me—and I told him a lot about you. He wouldn't make the offer if he didn't mean it. Preston—don't you see? This could be the answer. A new country, a new beginning. You've always wanted to travel. We could put everything behind us. (*Happily.*) Apart from anything else, they have wonderful weather out there. And look at this bit—at the end. (*Turns letter for him.*) He's even offered to advance our passage money, and we can pay him back later!

JIM. It's a very good offer.

GEORGIE. Very good! It's fabulous! (*She kneels beside him.*)

JIM. Mind you, I don't know about their timbers.

GEORGIE. You'd soon learn. I mean—you know how to organize the import and export of timber—that's what he has in mind. He says they're crying out for good men.

JIM. We couldn't go for quite a while.

GEORGIE. Why not?

JIM. Well—a divorce takes—

GEORGIE. We can go out there and get married later, when it comes through. What's to stop us? What's to stop us going next week, come to that?

JIM. Next week!

GEORGIE. Next month, then. The point is, we can go soon. We've got this to look forward to—

JIM. Suppose it didn't work out?

GEORGIE. Then you'd find something else. Australia is a big country— opening up all the time. This was waiting for me when I got home on Friday night. Lying on the mat. I don't know how I contained myself till this morning. I got the crazy idea of coming round to your house and making some excuse about the office—just so that I could tell you! Suddenly everything has a shape, a pattern, we know where we're heading. Shall I write and tell him that we—

JIM. No. Wait—

GEORGIE. I needn't give him a date—I can say we accept the offer, and will make arrangements as soon as possible. I want this for you, darling, even more than I want it for myself. I know what you can do, you see. I know that once you get a real chance—God, when I think of the years you've wasted at Simpson's— We mustn't wait too long—we've a lot of time to make up. (*Checks.*) Preston— don't you want me to write and accept?

JIM. Yes—

GEORGIE. Preston, what's the matter? I thought you'd be as excited as I am.

JIM. I am—only—there's such a lot of things to clear up, you see—

GEORGIE. You're thinking about Amy, aren't you?

JIM. Well, partly, yes. I'd have to come to some arrangement—I couldn't just sail off without— There's the question of money—

GEORGIE. I didn't suggest that you should just run off. I know you've got responsibilities, but this is the chance of a lifetime, Preston— what you've always dreamed of. You can't let it go—you mustn't!

JIM. I don't want to—

GEORGIE (*rising*). But there's Amy—

JIM. Yes.

(GEORGIE *moves* U.S.L.)

GEORGIE. You didn't speak to her last night, did you? You didn't tell her—

(*He shakes his head.*)

I knew. I knew the moment you came in.

JIM. I couldn't find the moment, Georgie—the right moment.

GEORGIE. No. You never can.

JIM. I wanted to. I was going to. The opportunity just didn't—just didn't come up. I have to pick the right time, Georgie.

GEORGIE (*with a shrug*). So—

JIM (*rises*). I'm sorry, Georgie.

GEORGIE (*fiercely*). I don't want you to be sorry! All I want is you to make up your mind what you want to do and do it!

JIM. You know what I want.

GEORGIE. How do I know? A dozen times you've said you'd speak to her; you've promised me a dozen times. Perhaps you prefer it like this—maybe it suits you to have two women, two beds.

JIM. Georgie! (*He moves towards her.*)

GEORGIE. I'm sorry—I didn't mean that. But I must know, Preston. That is the simple issue. I have to know about my life. I don't like pushing, but I have to know soon.

JIM. I will tell her, Georgie.

(GEORGIE *moves away to* D.S.R. *He is now facing her* C.S.)

GEORGIE. You know what shocks me about myself? Would you like to know? It isn't the fact that I'm a—a sort of Sunday woman, sleeping around with a married man. That doesn't shame me. No—I'm scared because I learned to lie and cheat so easily. All of a sudden I'm an expert at deceit. That time I met your wife I faced her without a flicker—I lied like a professional.

JIM. Don't talk like that, Georgie!

GEORGIE. Maybe you can take it—I can't. You know the worst thing for me? (*Her voice falls to a whisper.*) It is the thought of you at night with Amy—

JIM. Will you stop it!

GEORGIE. I can't help it, Preston. I've got a visual imagination; I see things too clearly. How can you do it? How can you go home and undress and climb into bed next to your wife an hour or so after you've been with me?

(*He stares at her, deeply hurt by her words, unable to answer. He turns away, but she goes to him, takes his hand quickly.*)

I'm sorry. Anyway, that shows you how I feel.

(*He twists her hand in his hands, nervously.*)

JIM. I've tried to tell Amy a dozen times. I've had the words on the tip of my tongue—and they've slipped back. It isn't easy, Georgie.

GEORGIE. Of course it's not easy! (*She pulls away from him, moves away.*) The easy way would be to leave it, let things drift on as they are. That would be terribly modern. Only I'm old-fashioned. I may not look it, but I'm an old-fashioned girl. I believe in morality. I'm twenty-three years old and until I met you I was a virgin. That's really old-fashioned. Was Amy a virgin when you met her—was she intact? I expect she was—so we're quits. (*She checks, continues less bitterly.*) I'm sorry. I didn't mean to be a bitch. Only when you say it isn't easy—God!

JIM. I only meant—she's so sure, you see, so certain. She lives as though each day is a holiday by the sea-side, as though nothing can touch her. She's innocent, like a child. When I do tell her—don't you see? It could break her.

GEORGIE. I'm not so sure. Sometimes I think the Amys of this world are unbreakable, indestructible. Preston, I feel sorry for her, too. Truthfully. But what else is there to do—what else? If you love me, if you're not lying to me.

JIM. Georgie!

GEORGIE. Then you have to make a decision. It isn't just Amy—it isn't just me. It's a decision about you—your whole life. Don't dodge this one, Preston, don't avoid this—

JIM. Tonight. I'll tell her tonight. I promise.

GEORGIE. No! Don't promise, don't make promises. Do it, that's all—do it.

JIM. I'll talk to her tonight. I'll get her to see it somehow. (*He goes to her.*) I do love you, Georgie. I'm not lying to you. You've changed everything for me—you know that? Until I met you I used to think that I'd had my share of life. It's the truth—I thought I was more or less finished. Oh, I didn't worry about it, or feel sorry for myself. I accepted it. I thought—well, this is what it is going to be like for the next thirty—forty—years. A few laughs, a few tears, a cigarette here, a drink there. I didn't expect much more than that. You changed it all, Georgie. You came into my life like a star.

(GEORGIE *suddenly clings to him in tears. Their embrace has an edge of desperation in it.*)

Don't cry—don't cry any more. Don't cry. I'll tell her tonight—I'll settle it once and for all.

CURTAIN

SCENE 3

The PRESTON *living-room, that evening.* AMY, *iron in hand, is standing by some unfinished ironing at an ironing-board* L. *of table. She is now wearing a dress. The gramophone is playing the lament from "I Pagliacci" by Leoncavallo. Slumped in the armchair* R. *is* HILDA, *a neighbour. She is a blonde, pretty little cockney, usually cheerful, though at this moment she is rather down.*

HILDA. I mean—all those years we spent—

AMY. Sh—sh—

(HILDA *subsides impatiently for a moment or two until the chorus ends.* AMY *sighs deeply.*)

Ah—I think that's so wonderful. Did you like it, Hilda?

HILDA. Mmm? Oh—yes—all right.

AMY. It's from an opera. This clown is heartbroken, you see, but he still has to go before the people and make them laugh. His heart is aching with sorrow but he has to make them laugh.

HILDA. Why?

AMY. Well, that's show-business. I mean—the show must go on.

HILDA. But why has he got a broken heart?

AMY. I don't know. I've never seen the opera. One day I'm going to make Jimbo take me to see the whole thing.

HILDA. You always been so mad about music, Amy?

AMY (*laughing*). Since the day I was born. Jimbo says music is an obsession with me. I suppose he's right. I tell him—you thank your lucky stars I'm not a drinker. Do you know what my mother told me once? She said—this is what she said—she said "Music is the smile on the face of the human race".

HILDA. I only like music you can dance to.

AMY. I like any kind. Dancing music. (*She hums a tune and dances a few steps.*) Marching music. (*She tum-tums a march and parades a few paces.*) Singing music—and church music—and oh, anything so long as it's got a real tune. Music is company—like a friend in the house—you know?

HILDA. You're a case.

AMY (*smiling*). I know.

HILDA. Amy, do you think I'm being unreasonable about Willie?

(AMY *resumes ironing.*)

AMY. I don't know, lovey. Seems to me he's a good man.

HILDA. He doesn't have to be so bloody-minded, does he? He never takes me into consideration at all.

AMY. He works hard—he studies. He doesn't do that just for himself— it's for you, and the baby— You can't ask more of a man.

HILDA. There's got to be some limit. I mean—six years we danced together, trying to reach perfection. We won sixteen dance contests in six years. We had managers on their knees, begging us to turn professional. Not Willie. Oh no. He wants a normal life, he says. A normal life! He won't even take me dancing one night a week!

(AMY *laughs.* HILDA *rises and goes* U.S. *of table, near* AMY.)

You can laugh. Believe me, it isn't funny. He comes home and sticks his head in those books and I don't get a word out of him. The other night—the other night—you know what I did? I got so mad, I stripped off there and then, in the living-room right in front of him.

AMY. You didn't!

HILDA. Oh yes, I did. I was determined to get some attention. The whole lot came off. I stood there, like Venus on a rock-cake, waiting for him to notice. Know what happened? He looked up and saw me and he said: "You going to have a bath?" Then he went right on studying. (*In disgust.*) That's what he calls living a normal life!

AMY. It's always a bad time when a man is trying to make his way in the world. All his wife can do is sit back and be patient and try and help. It will pass.

HILDA. Yes. By that time I'll be too old to worry! (*She crosses and sits in armchair.*)

AMY. Men see these things different, lovey. To them the job is everything. Take Jimbo—I mean, the way he works— (*Suddenly.*) Oh! Jimbo—he'll be in soon—his supper—it's cooking—but I should have checked it— Excuse me—

(*She rushes out to the kitchen. The door opens and* WILLIE *looks in. This is* HILDA's *husband, a light, tired man of about 28.*)

WILLIE. Oh, you're here.

HILDA. Well?

WILLIE. The baby's crying.

HILDA. You're his father.

WILLIE. I can't do anything with him. You'd better come.

HILDA. Men! Helpless! (*She gets up angrily, moves to door.*)

WILLIE. I've told you before—you spend too much time with Amy. Do you want to get like her?

HILDA. Amy is a good friend! At least she speaks to me. At least she notices that I'm a living person.

(*She goes out.* WILLIE *is about to follow her when* AMY *re-enters and goes* U.S. *of table.*)

AMY. Phew—just in time. It's all right. Oh, Willie—it's you.

WILLIE. Hilda's gone back. The baby's crying.

AMY. He's all right? Nothing I can do?

WILLIE. No, he's just hungry, I think. (*He turns to go.*)

AMY. Willie—

(*He turns back, comes down a little.*)

WILLIE. Yes?

AMY. Willie, it's really none of my business. But Hilda was talking to me just now. She's pretty low. She needs cheering up. Could you— I mean—why don't you skip your books tonight and take her out somewhere—

WILLIE. Did she ask you to ask me?

AMY. No, of course not—

WILLIE. But she was telling you how neglected she is!

AMY. She just said you were always busy, that's all.

WILLIE (*stiffly*). Well, you were right first time. It isn't any of your business. I'd be obliged if you'd keep out of it.

AMY. Willie, don't get offended. I'm only speaking in a friendly way —out of friendship.

WILLIE (*angrily*). Every time she wants to let off steam she comes running to you. I'm asking you not to encourage her, Amy. Things are tough enough already.

AMY. She's young, Willie. She doesn't understand. She just needs— you know—a little attention.

WILLIE. I could do with a little attention, too—a little appreciation. It isn't all on one side, you know. Just let us run our own lives, that's all I ask.

(JIM *enters*.)

JIM. Evening, Willie.

WILLIE. Evening, Jim. Excuse me. Night, Amy. (*Exit*.)

AMY. Night.

JIM. What was all that about?

(AMY *goes to him, gives him a little peck*.)

AMY. I don't know—honestly, I don't.

JIM. What was he on his hind legs about, then?

(*He moves to just above armchair* R. *and takes off coat*.)

AMY. Hilda was in here. He thought maybe I'd been—you know— interfering.

JIM (*tersely*). You want to keep out of it.

AMY. But I do, Jimbo. I don't interfere. I'm the last person—

JIM. Nothing worse than somebody else interfering—

AMY (*mildly exasperated*). But, Jimbo, I didn't say a word. Honestly, I mean—what can I do? The girl comes in here, she tells me all her troubles—

JIM. You shouldn't listen.

AMY (*smiling*). Oh, Jimbo.

JIM. I mean it. You've enough to do in your own home, without try- ing to run theirs.

(*She takes his coat and moves* U.S. *to door with it*.)

AMY. I don't know. You try to help people, to be sympathetic—and it's all thrown up in your face.

JIM. I've told you before—you're too free with your advice. You go round handing it out all the time. I've told you before. (*He is pushing this too hard, partly to cover his own guilt at what he has to do*.)

AMY (*quietly*). All right, Jimbo.

JIM. In the long run they only resent it.

AMY (*tetchily*). All right, Jimbo, all right.

JIM (*too reasonably*). And don't get sulky about it. I'm only telling you for your own good. If you can't be spoken to—

AMY. Jimbo—could we forget it?

JIM. Sure. I don't want to make a book out of it. I was only saying— for your own good. If people tell you their troubles—don't com- ment. Just don't comment. That's the best way.

(*She sighs, takes coat out to hall. She comes back to* U.S. *of table.
There is a little silence as he looks for a newspaper and she hangs his
jacket on a chair. Then, seeing his tired and worried face,* AMY *smiles.
She can never be down for long. She goes to him.*)

AMY. Now—you sit down. I'm going to put your supper on a tray
and you can eat it in the armchair.

JIM. I don't know that I'm too hungry, Amy.

AMY (*disappointed*). Oh, Jimbo—

JIM (*quickly*). I'll do my best.

AMY. That's good. Now you sit there. I bet you didn't stop for lunch.
I bet you worked right through.

JIM. I did; I—I had a good lunch.

AMY. Not as nice as what I've got for you!

(*He sits in the armchair. She brings a can of beer from the top of the
bureau. She holds it behind her back.*)

Cup of tea while you're waiting?

JIM. Please.

AMY. Got something better than tea. Here! (*She hands him the can.*)

JIM. How much money do you want to borrow, eh? All this fuss!

AMY. I've got a good husband, a good son and a nice home. Sometimes I like to show that I appreciate my good fortune. I'll get your
food.

(*As she hurries to the door:*)

JIM. Where's the opener?

AMY. Opener? Oh—can-opener—can-opener—now where—

JIM. All right—I'll find it.

(*She goes to the kitchen. He crosses to bureau* U.S.R. *and rummages
around in a drawer that is packed with stuff, finds an opener, and pierces
the can. He pours the beer into a glass, takes a swig.*)

(*Calls.*) Amy, do you mind if we don't go out tonight?

AMY (*from kitchen offstage*). Oh! I was looking forward— (*Pause.*) If
you don't feel like it, Jimbo, we'll stay in.

JIM. I'll go out if you want.

AMY (*from kitchen*). No. No. We'll have a quiet evening on our own.

(JIM *sits in armchair. He leans back wearily, his eyes closed.*
AMY *returns with a laden tray.*)

Jimbo! (*With pride.*) All ready. No waiting. Well, only a minute.
I made up my mind tonight it would be ready and waiting. (*She
crosses to armchair.*)

JIM. Service!

AMY. I made up my mind. Steak—medium rare. French fried pota-
toes. Chips really, but tonight we'll call them French fried— Apple
pie to follow, with fresh cream. Fresh cream. (*Hands tray to him.*)

JIM. What about the tomato sauce?
> (*She goes to bureau and brings tomato sauce down to him. He takes a liberal helping of this.*)

Good!

AMY. Oh, I can do it. If I set my heart to do something, I can usually do it. (*She crosses and switches on radio. Then she throws some newspapers from a chair, draws it up near him, ready to share his enjoyment.*) Now—eat. Eat it all up.

JIM. What about you?

AMY. I've had mine. I mean—I don't want anything more.
> (*He starts to eat as she watches anxiously.*)

All right?

JIM. Fine.

AMY. I tried a new way with the chips. What you do is cook them for a minute or so, and then take them out of the pan. You leave them for another minute, and then put them back.

JIM. What does that do?

AMY. It makes them nice and crisp. Don't you think it makes them crisp?

JIM. Yes.
> (*She leans across, takes chip from his plate, dips it in salt on edge of plate, and eats it thoughtfully.*)

AMY. I cut them smaller, too. I mean—they're nicer when they're small. More taste. (*She puts her head back and listens to the radio.*) That's Tchaikovsky. The "Pathetique". It makes me want to cry, you know that? It's so sad.

JIM. Yes.

AMY. A man who can write music like that—I mean—when he sat down and wrote that—how much sadness he must have had in his heart.

JIM. Amy—switch it off.

AMY. Don't you like it?

JIM. Not in the mood. Switch it off.

AMY. Yes, it is too sad. Shall I find something else?

JIM. No. No—give the radio a rest, please.

AMY. All right, dear. (*She crosses to bureau and after a moment's hesitation switches off.*) Jimbo—you'll have to speak to your son, you know that? You'll have to speak to him very seriously. (*She crosses to ironing-board L. and starts to fold clothes.*)

JIM. Why—what's he been saying?

AMY. It's incredible. The ideas! Do you know what he asked me today—what he actually asked me?

JIM. Well?

AMY. He asked me if you and I ever—well—went away together before we were married. (*She giggles.*) Honestly!

JIM. What!

AMY. It's the truth. He said he didn't mean it in a personal way. He just wanted to know—something to do with a speech he has to make.

JIM. He's making a speech on that?

AMY. Well, not exactly on that. I mean—not just about us. It's a sort of debate on—on—I'll remember in a minute—on—I know: "Are young people today less moral than their parents were?" That's it!

JIM. A good question! What did you tell him?

AMY. What do you think! I told him he had no business to ask such questions.

JIM. Was he satisfied?

AMY. No. So I told him the answer was definitely no. Your father had too much respect for me to do any such thing—that's what I said.

JIM. And did that satisfy him?

AMY. Yes. As a matter of fact, I think he was rather pleased. Underneath it all, he's really very conventional. You think I said the right thing?

JIM. If it satisfied him—yes.

AMY. I know we've always said we'd tell him the exact truth about everything—but in this case—I mean, I think I was justified. You can take freedom too far.

JIM. I'll speak to him. He can't go around asking people questions like that!

AMY. Oh, he doesn't mean anything by it, Jimbo. He's a serious boy. We don't know how lucky we are. Honestly—when you read about some boys, the way they behave. Brian's a serious boy and he's growing into a fine man. (*She crosses and sits in chair beside him.*)

JIM. Just the same—he must be told. There are some things you don't ask.

AMY (*with a little laugh*). I wonder if he would be shocked—I mean, if I'd told him that we did go away together—several times—before we were married.

JIM. You won't tell him anything!

AMY. Jimbo! What do you take me for? Of course I shan't. Not that I'm ashamed, mind you.

JIM. It's a long time ago. We were a couple of kids.

AMY (*smiling, remembering*). Oh yes! We were so young! I was nineteen— (*Suddenly.*) Jimbo—I've just thought. It won't be long before Brian is that age!

JIM. Two years to go yet.

AMY. All the same, I hope he doesn't—well—(*Smiles.*) If he does, I don't suppose he will tell us. We didn't tell our parents, after all. (*Remembering again.*) You know, Jimbo, I still think of that farm in Suffolk. We spent a whole week there—remember? I think it's my most treasured memory. At first, I was petrified. Honestly—I was petrified. I thought everyone was staring at us, as if they knew we had a guilty secret. And I was frightened that—well—that I would disappoint you—you know. You were the first man in my life—I didn't know a thing—I was so anxious to make you happy. You were happy, weren't you, Jimbo?

 (*He is embarrassed by all this—rather ashamed by the recollection of his early love for* AMY. *He tries to play it light.*)

JIM. As far as I can remember.

AMY. Oh, Jimbo! (*Chattering on.*) Well, I know you were happy. And I'm not ashamed. I mean, we loved each other—there's nothing shameful in that. Funny—my mother always said I should go out with lots of boys before I decided on a husband. But I picked you right away—I never went out with anyone else. You were the first man in my life. No, definitely, I'm not ashamed. If St. Peter holds it against me when I report at the pearly gates, I shall give him a piece of my mind!

 (JIM *passes her the tray with an abrupt movement.*)

(*Anxiously.*) You haven't eaten it!

JIM. I've had all I want.

AMY. Did I burn the steak? Was it tough?

JIM. It was fine, Amy! It's just that I'm not hungry. I've got past it.

 (*She puts tray on table and goes to the radio to switch it on, then remembers and stops.*)

AMY. Would you like to watch some television?

JIM. No.

AMY. All right. We'll just sit quietly and have a nice conversation.

 (*She sits near him. She smiles at him, waiting for him to start the conversation. He makes an effort.*)

JIM. What have you been doing today?

AMY. Oh, I've been pretty busy—you know. Actually I've hardly sat down a minute. I don't know where the time goes to.

JIM. You've been busy. What exactly have you done? Tell me.

AMY (*amused by his obtuseness*). Tell me, he says! You think this home runs itself? One day I'd like to make a record of the miles I walk around this place. From here to the kitchen, back again, into the bedroom, back again—you add all that up, and it would work out like a—like a real marathon. I've hardly been off my feet all day. I think the only time I sat down was to make my entry in that contest.

JIM (*irritably*). Amy—those contests are a waste of time and money.

AMY. You wouldn't say that if I won a prize. Do you know what the first prize is worth? £5,000! Imagine—£5,000! And it's so easy. I mean—they give you this list of household articles, you see—and you have to put them in order of importance. And there's something else, Jimbo. You know I'm a subject of Capricorn. Well—it says in the same paper that this is a lucky week for all subjects of Capricorn. You see? (*She smiles in triumph.*)

JIM (*harshly*). Every week there's a new contest—and every week you think up a new reason why you're going to win it. Get it into your head, Amy—you won't win, not if you live to be a hundred and one.

AMY (*a little hurt, surprised*). How can you be so sure, Jimbo? Someone's got to win, after all.

JIM. Not us. Not us. We're not the type.

AMY. Oh—you're as bad as Brian. He's just as cynical. But I've got faith. One day—

JIM (*angrily*). One day! It'll never come, Amy. Grow up. You're not a child any more. You're just wasting time and money! (*He gets up, moves around table restlessly.*)

AMY. It only costs a shilling to enter. We won't miss a shilling, Jimbo.

JIM. If you spent a bit more time keeping this place tidy, I wouldn't mind so much. Look at it! Look at it! (*He sweeps a pile of clothes from the table.*) To come home once and find the place half-way tidy! Just once! Have you finished the ironing?

AMY (*bewildered*). Not yet. Jimbo, sit down. You're tired. You haven't finished your beer.

JIM (*fiercely*). Either finish the damn ironing or put it away. Just once to come home and find the place tidy! You've got time for Hilda, time for your damned music, time for everything—except the things that matter! I'm sick and tired of telling you—sick and bloody tired! Just once to find this place tidy! Just once!

(*He strides into the bedroom, slams the door. AMY sits there, hurt and puzzled. She frowns. She hesitates whether to follow him, decides against it. She takes a potato chip from his plate, pops it into her mouth, wipes her fingers on the side of her dress—every move mechanical. He comes back, still angry, strides to the armchair where he has left his cigarettes. She gets up warily, moves to U.S. of table, watching him.*)

AMY. There's no need to shout at me, Jimbo. What's wrong, what is it?

JIM. I've told you. I'm sick of telling you! The way we live—the way we live!

AMY. That Simpson! He's upset you! I can tell. In the next world he'll have a lot to answer for.

JIM. It isn't Simpson! For Christ's sake, Amy. Open your eyes. Look around at this—this pig-sty! It isn't Simpson! (*He almost shouts this. He moves back to bedroom, pauses, and the anger goes out of him. He turns.*). Amy—listen—I want you to listen.

AMY. You don't have to shout to make me hear, Jimbo.

JIM. I know. I'm sorry. I didn't mean— (*He stops wearily. He closes his eyes for a moment, smoothes his hair.*)

AMY. You're right, Jimbo—I know you're right. I don't defend myself. I try and get the place looking straight and somehow—I don't know. I'm sorry, Jimbo. You have a right to come home to something better.

JIM (*forcing the words*). It's not you, Amy. I didn't mean to shout. I'm not blaming you.

AMY. Then you should. You've been too easy-going with me. You're like that with everyone.

JIM. It's not your fault, Amy.

(*She moves to him.*)

AMY. Of course it is. But I promise you—this time I will make a real effort to get organized. I know I've said it before, but this time I mean it. I don't say this to excuse myself, Jimbo—but Mrs. Beeny told me something the day before yesterday that opened my eyes. I know what's wrong with me. I've got mineral deficiency—that's lack of iron in my blood. She's going to get me a jar of black molasses, and she says, if I eat two tablespoonfuls every day—

JIM (*cutting across her, desperately*). Amy—I want you to divorce me. I want a divorce.

AMY. Jimbo!

JIM. You've got to divorce me, Amy. (*He sighs as though an enormous load has been lifted from his shoulders.*)

AMY. You're joking—

JIM. No. No, Amy. For weeks I've been trying to tell you, for months.

AMY (*desperately*). You're always playing jokes, Jimbo—you're always joking.

JIM. I'm not joking, Amy.

(*She looks down at the tray, picks it up. She takes it through to the kitchen. She comes back. She gives him a stricken glance, and starts to tidy the room, picking up ironing. He crosses to her, takes her arm gently.*)

Leave that, Amy.

AMY. Leave it? You said—

JIM. Leave it. Sit down a moment.

AMY. Sit down? No—Jimbo, you meant it—you really meant what you said?

JIM (*gently*). Amy—look, sit down. We've got to talk.

(*She sits mechanically in chair* U.S. *centre of table, her eyes never leaving their restless search of his face.*)

AMY. Jimbo—you wouldn't joke about a thing like this—

JIM. Amy, please—

AMY. Is it because of the place?

JIM. No—no—no.

AMY. If you're trying to punish me, Jimbo—if it's that—

JIM (*gently*). That's the last thing, Amy—the last thing I want to do. (*He sits* R. *at table.*)

AMY. Then why? If it isn't because of the place—(*She looks at him steadily.*) You've found someone else. Is that it? That must be the reason.

(*He nods. She tears the next words out in anguish.*)

No—oh, Jimbo—no—no!

JIM. I'm sorry, Amy.

AMY (*incredulous*). Sorry?

JIM. It's not much to say, I know that, but I am. I am truly sorry.

AMY. You read about this happening to other people. You never think —one day it could be your own story. (*A pause, then:*) Who is it? Is it Georgie?

JIM. Yes.

AMY. Georgie. (*She turns her head away in anguish.*)

JIM. No one's to blame, Amy. No one. You've met her. She's no home-breaker, you know that. All this just—well, it just happened.

AMY. Every day you read in the paper about this happening to other people. (*Quickly.*) Jimbo—what about Brian? Have you thought about Brian—what will he say?

JIM. He's old enough to understand.

AMY (*bitterly*). Is he? I'm his mother—and I don't understand.

JIM. It's not just Georgie, Amy. It's not simply that. At my time of life a man doesn't go for a girl just because she's pretty.

AMY. She is pretty. I said that to you after I met her the first time. She's pretty—she has very good legs—I always said that. And she's young.

JIM. It isn't just Georgie. I'm trying to tell you, to explain—

AMY. I'd like you to explain, Jimbo. I'd like to know.

JIM. It's a question of my whole life. I feel as if I'm living in a tunnel. I've got to—

W.D.G.—C

AMY (*cutting in, full of her own thoughts*). You were with her today?

JIM. Yes.

AMY. You didn't go to the office at all?

JIM. No.

AMY. All those other Sundays—those evenings—

JIM. I was with Georgie.

AMY. You lied to me—you told me a pack of lies.

JIM. Amy—

AMY. You lied to Brian, too. Is that what she's done for you? You never told that boy a lie, you never told him an intentional lie in your life.

JIM (*rising in agitation*). Amy! Will you let me tell you?

AMY. I'm sorry.

JIM (*he moves around restlessly*). I'm trying to explain. You see— I mean— I'm a young man still—I'm not old—but I'm going nowhere. I feel I'm—I'm stuck in a lift between two floors. Do you understand what I mean? We live a mile from Tower Bridge, a mile from the river, but we might as well be on an island in the middle of nowhere. The whole world comes and goes a mile from here, and we don't even look out of the window!

AMY. You mean, I hold you back. Is that what you mean? I'm a burden to you.

JIM. No. It's not that.

AMY. What else? I'm a drag on you, a chain around your throat. But Georgie, she's younger, she's got brains, she's educated. With her behind you, you could get ahead, make your way.

JIM. No. That's not the way to put it, Amy—face up to it. We haven't been happy together.

AMY (*incredulous*). Jimbo! How can you make such a statement? We've hardly had one quarrel in all our married life! (*She rises, goes to him.*)

JIM (*desperate, angry*). I'm trying to say this without hurting you!

AMY (*fiercely*). Say it! You hurt me enough—a few more words won't matter!

JIM. Then listen! Listen! (*But as he looks at her hurt face his anger subsides.*)

AMY. Well?

JIM. Leave it. We'll talk tomorrow. Tomorrow we'll discuss the whole thing.

AMY. No. No, Jimbo. You left it long enough. Tell me what's wrong. I'm entitled to know. You said we hadn't been happy. I don't understand that, Jimbo. I've been happy—since the day I met you I've been happy. I never knew you felt like this. I never guessed.

What did I do? Why weren't you happy, Jimbo? I must know. I must know now!
> (*We hear the murmur of voices, of laughter, the sound of a key in a lock.* AMY *starts in fear.*)
Brian! It's Brian. What shall we say to him—what are we going to do?

JIM. We'll talk later. Sh—sh—
> (*They try to compose themselves.* AMY *smooths her dress, dabs at her eyes.* JIM *takes a cigarette.* BRIAN *enters with* CHRISTINE, PAUL *and* SHIRLEY—*three of his friends.*)

BRIAN. Hi! You were supposed to be going out!
> (*He wrinkles his face in mock disappointment. There are general greetings to which* AMY *and* JIM *respond as best they can.* BRIAN *gives* JIM *a light.*)
We got some records we want to play over, Mum. You'll like 'em.

AMY. Nice.

CHRISTINE. This one's fabulous—way up in the charts, fabulous; you must hear it.

BRIAN. Don't talk so much. Let's hear it!

CHRISTINE (*with a smile*). Get him! (*She goes to the gramophone with the records and prepares to play them.*)

JIM. Your mother's got a headache, Brian.

AMY. No—no—it's all right. Go ahead.

BRIAN. You sure, Mum? You do look a bit whacked.

AMY. I'm fine. Go ahead.

BRIAN (*smiling, kidding them*). You two been arguing? (*To the others.*) What do you know? I mean—you can't trust your parents these days. The moment you turn your back, they start an argument.

CHRISTINE. Do you allow him to speak to you like that, Mr. Preston?

JIM (*forcing a smile*). He's stronger than I am, Christine.

PAUL. Him? One punch and he's finished. He couldn't knock the skin off a rice pudding.

BRIAN. You're asking for it, man—and will you get it!
> (*He advances on* PAUL. *The other kids yell encouragement. They spar lightly.*)

KIDS. Seconds out!
I'll take odds on the big 'un.
Let's see some real action—
Come out fighting—
Kill him, Brian, kill him.
> (*Etc. ad lib.*)
> (AMY *winces at the noise.* CHRISTINE *imposes herself above it all.*)

CHRISTINE. Quiet! Quiet! Do you want to hear this, or don't you? Quiet!

(They subside.)

BRIAN. I'll take you later, man.

PAUL. You'll be lucky.

CHRISTINE. Sh—sh— *(She starts the music.)*

BRIAN. This is the real stuff, Mum. You got any devils—this will shake 'em loose!

(The music begins. It is a noisy recording of the latest pop hit.) Turn it up, Christine. Let's hear it, for Pete's sake.

The noisy words of the number fill the room. The youngsters join in the rhythm. They become so absorbed they do not notice AMY get up and move towards the bedroom. JIM intercepts her, but she shakes him off silently. The music seems to grow louder, louder. The lights fade until we have a single spot on AMY, clutching the framework of the door for support, weeping bitterly.

CURTAIN

ACT TWO

SCENE I

The lights fade in on the PRESTON *living-room. It is tidier than we have ever seen it. We can hear a great clatter of pans from the direction of the kitchen.*

It is morning.

AMY, *in her old dressing-gown, comes bustling in from the kitchen. She pauses, looking around, pressing the tips of her fingers against her mouth as she wonders if she has left anything undone. She catches sight of a heap of magazines on the floor. She picks these up and takes them* U.S.R. *to cupboard. As she opens the door, a lot of tightly packed stuff falls out. With a murmur of exasperation she presses the whole lot back inside, together with the magazines, and closes the door.*

Then she proceeds to set the table for breakfast, putting on plates, dishes, etc. She spills some salt, clicks her gums in irritation, and taking a pinch of the spilled salt, throws it over her right shoulder. She notices a mark on one of the plates and rubs it on the sleeve of her robe.

She is surprisingly cheerful. In fact, typical AMY *fashion, she has almost convinced herself that what happened the previous evening was simply an outburst against her untidy ways. She feels that she has only to put one or two things right and be reasonable and it will all blow over. She still can't believe* JIM *would ever leave her.*

BRIAN *comes in* U.S.C. *whistling. He stops short as he sees the room.* AMY *waits for his reaction with anxious pride.*

BRIAN. Stone me—I must be in the wrong house! (*He turns, teasingly, to go out.*)

AMY. Brian!

(*He comes back, shaking his head. He goes to her, above table, still teasing, examines her face carefully. He turns her round, rubs his chin as though puzzled.*)

BRIAN. Yes—you are my mother all right. Must be the right place. What's happened? Must have been an earthquake during the night!

AMY. Don't be so saucy, young man! (*Proudly.*) I've been up since five o'clock, tidying round.

BRIAN. Ah—one of your annual bursts.

AMY (*hurt*). Brian!

(*He embraces her, laughing.*)

BRIAN. I'm kidding. Can't you take a joke? It looks great, Mum, great.

AMY. I can do it. When I set my mind to it I can do it. From now on things are going to be different around here. A place for everything and everything in its place.

BRIAN (*moves across to bureau*). I left a book in here last night.

AMY. What was it called? I did see a book lying around.

BRIAN. Blue cover—called "Darrow for the Defence". Paul loaned it to me. I left it on the table.

AMY. You shouldn't leave your things lying about. Serves you right if you lose them.

BRIAN (*aggrieved*). Turn it up, Mum! Coming from you—crikey!

AMY. I told you, there's going to be big changes in this house. The proper place for your books is in your room.

BRIAN. O.K. O.K. So we have a new régime. But before I can put it in my room I've got to find it.

AMY. I put a lot of books and papers in that cupboard. It might be in there. No—no—wait! I'll look. I don't want everything upset. (*She crosses quickly to cupboard. She opens the door of the cupboard carefully, rummages inside with one hand and eventually produces the book.*) This it?

BRIAN. That's the one.

(*She fastens the cupboard door carefully.* BRIAN *riffles through the book, moving down to fireplace.* AMY *goes back to table.*)

You know, Mum, I think I might like to take up the law as a career.

AMY (*preoccupied*). What, dear?

(BRIAN *pins her with an accusing forefinger, moves in to her like an American district attorney.*)

BRIAN. And where, may I ask, were you on the night of the murder, Mrs. Preston? Don't prevaricate, I warn you. I shall call witnesses whose evidence will prove—prove, I say—that on that night you were seen making your way to the Red Barn with an axe in your hand! Do you deny it? Do you?

AMY. Not now, dear. I'm busy. What was I going to do? Ah, yes—cups—cups—

(*She sets some cups on the table.* BRIAN *sighs. He has a sudden, youthful depression. He drops into chair* L. *of table.*)

BRIAN. Trouble is, by tonight I shall think of something else I want to do. I can't seem to stay with anything for more than a day. I'm not a very stable character.

AMY. You're young, Brian, there's time.

BRIAN (*impatiently*). Being young has nothing to do with it, Mum. You make my age sound like a sickness or something, as if it gives me the right to be feeble-minded.

AMY (*mildly surprised and out of her depth*). I didn't say anything of the kind. Honestly, the words you put into my mouth. I simply said that you're young. Isn't that a fact—what do you call it?—an indisputable fact.

BRIAN. A fact, yes. Being young is a fact, not an excuse. It doesn't make me into a special kind of animal. People of your age use the words "young" and "juvenile" and "teenager" and—oh, things like that like earplugs.

AMY (*smiling*). Like what?

BRIAN. Earplugs. You use 'em to stop your ears. Nowadays, if a feller is in his teens, he belongs to a special race. Who created this new species? We didn't. Next thing you know, the Government will be herding us into reservations.

AMY (*smiling*). You know, Brian, I think perhaps you should try and be a lawyer. Honestly, I'm not joking. You have a wonderful talent for words, you really have.

BRIAN. No. When I get excited—you know—I stutter, I fall over my words.

AMY. Oh, that's hardly noticeable now. You're much better than you used to be. And you're still you—(*She bites back the word "young".*) I nearly said it! (*Smiles.*) I nearly said you are still young. Oh!

BRIAN (*laughing*). Mum—I love you.

AMY (*lightly*). I'm glad somebody does. (*With a sad little smile, as though remembering.*) I'm very glad to hear that somebody cares!

(*She ruffles his hair lightly and goes into the kitchen. JIM comes in from the bedroom dressed for the office.*)

BRIAN. Hi, Dad.

JIM. Morning, son.

BRIAN. Watch your step around here, Dad. Mum's instituted a new régime.

(*JIM sits in armchair, tying shoes. BRIAN rises, puts book on table and crosses to JIM.*)

JIM. So I see.

BRIAN. Don't worry—it won't last long. We'll be back to normal within twenty-four hours. I guarantee it.

JIM. Don't mock your mother, Brian.

BRIAN (*protesting mildly*). I wasn't mocking her, Dad. Cripes—she's unique among women. I was just stating a simple indisputable fact.

JIM. All right. But just remember—she is your mother.

BRIAN (*lightly*). I shan't forget, Dad.

JIM. And there's no need to answer back all the time.

BRIAN. Dad—I just said—

JIM. You're too damn free with your answers! And your questions, too, come to that. Once or twice lately I've been meaning to speak to you.

BRIAN. About what?

JIM. Never mind. It doesn't matter.

BRIAN (*logically*). But it does matter—you just said so.

JIM (*with growing irritation*). Look, Brian—we've been pretty easy with you. Maybe too easy. All I'm saying is—watch this! (*He taps his mouth with a finger.*) Watch it. Don't take advantage.

BRIAN. Yes. O.K. I got the message. (*He moves back to table, picks up book.*)

JIM. And don't take that attitude either. Don't try and play the martyr.

BRIAN (*wearily*). I'm not taking any attitude. I just said—okay, message received and understood.

JIM. You must always have the last word! You must always have the last bloody word!

(BRIAN *looks at him for a moment. Then he shrugs, and goes to his room.* JIM *looks up and sees* AMY *standing in the kitchen entrance. She has heard part of this exchange. He feels ashamed of his outburst, and knows the real reason for it, but he tries to cover up. He rises and starts to knot his tie.*)

That boy goes too far. He's got to be checked.

AMY. Tea's all ready, Jimbo. (*She takes the pot to the table, starts to pour.*)

JIM. He's got an answer for everything. You can't speak to him without he's got an answer. (*He crosses to chair* R. *of table.*) We've been too easy with him. He's not grown-up yet! There's a limit!

(*Their eyes meet. There is a moment of awkwardness. He sits at table, chair* R. *She pours him a cup of tea.*)

AMY. You didn't sleep.

JIM. Not much.

AMY. Neither did I. I could feel you lying awake. I got up before five.

JIM. I heard you.

AMY. I've been working solid since five o'clock. Did you notice?

JIM. Yes—oh, yes—

AMY. I can do it, you see. When I put my mind to something I can do it.

JIM. Sure. I've always said that. I've always told people that.

(*She sits at table* C., *talking quickly as though trying to get things back to normal.*)

AMY. Do you know my chief failing, Jimbo? I've just realized. My chief failing is lack of concentration. I start things, but I don't finish them. My mind hops about from one thing to another like a bird. (*Smiles.*) I suppose that's why they call people like me bird-brain. (*Seriously.*) Still, they say if you understand your weakness, then you're half-way to curing it. Isn't that so?

JIM. So they say. Yes.

AMY. There's a course of lessons I could take. I've seen it advertised somewhere. Do you know, hundreds of famous people—famous people, mind you—have the same weakness. They took these lessons and it made all the difference. If I can develop my powers of concentration—

JIM (*rising*). I must go, Amy.

AMY (*anxiously*). No—wait—I wanted to ask you—I mean, we haven't talked. Jimbo, I was thinking about it all last night. I've made a plan, Jimbo. I've thought it over very carefully. We'll work it out right—do you understand? I mean, we've had problems before and we've got over them. I know we can work this out, I know we can.

JIM. Amy—I meant what I said last night.

AMY (*rising, goes to him*). Yes, yes—I know you did, Jimbo. And I understand, believe me, I completely understand. All I'm saying is, we're sensible people and there's Brian to consider—and everything —so if we both decide to work it out somehow—I know where I went wrong now, you see.

JIM (*cutting in, gently*). Amy, you're not listening. You're not listening. I meant what I said last night.

AMY (*desperately, deliberately, shutting out his words*). What I mean to say is—what I'm trying to get you to see, Jimbo, is—well, it's twenty years! Do you realize that? We've been together twenty years. If we got through that, Jimbo, there's surely no reason why—

JIM (*cutting in*). Amy, we can't discuss it now.

AMY. I know, I know. I'm just asking you to think it over, Jimbo. I mean, think it all over again. If you would give it another chance— I know I could alter, Jimbo, I know that.

JIM. Amy, look—

AMY. Your mind can't be finally made up, or you wouldn't have taken so long to tell me. That's reasonable, isn't it? Everybody has their ups and downs, Jimbo. The Wallaces were going to split up, remember? They worked it out all right. If they can do it— (*She is desperate for some kind of reassurance, some straw to cling to.*)

JIM. It's no good talking now, Amy. We'll go over the whole thing tonight.

AMY. But you will think about what I said? That's all I'm asking. Don't close your mind, Jimbo. Please. It isn't much to ask.

JIM. Amy, I must go. (*He moves* U.S. *towards door.*)

AMY. Wait. Jimbo. I want you to bring her home with you tonight. I want you to bring Georgie back so that we can all talk. Like—like civilized people. (*She moves up to him.*)

JIM. Amy! That's impossible. This is between us.

AMY. No! She's involved, too. If we could talk it over, if the three of us could only talk it over together, I'm sure—

JIM (*cutting in*). I can't ask her.

AMY. Why? Why not? Is she ashamed to face me?

JIM. No—it's not that. But it wouldn't be fair—

AMY. I just want to talk to her. I shan't make a scene, I promise. I just want us to talk like civilized people. At least ask her, Jimbo. Ask her. Tell her I'd like her to come back with you tonight to see me. Will you do that? Will you ask her?

JIM (*with a sigh*). I'll ask her—I'll tell her what you said.

AMY. That's all I want.

JIM. But don't bank on it. Don't bank on her coming.

AMY. As long as you ask her, that's all.

(BRIAN *comes in; they move apart.*)

JIM. Amy, I must go. So long, son.

BRIAN. 'Bye, Dad.

(JIM *moves to the door, pauses.*)

JIM (*awkwardly*). Sorry I sounded off at you, Brian. Didn't sleep too well. Didn't mean it. Sorry.

BRIAN (*smiling*). Okay, Dad. I'm sorry, too. I argue too much.

JIM. Fine. Be seeing you then.

BRIAN. Yes. See you.

(JIM *moves off.* BRIAN *crosses to table, sits in chair* L.)

AMY. Jimbo!

(*He pauses. She goes to him, holds up her face for the routine kiss he has given her at this time for twenty years. He kisses her cheek.*) Take care of yourself. Mind how you go.

JIM. 'Bye.

AMY. Make sure you get a good hot lunch.

JIM. I will.

AMY. And remember—you promised. You promised to think about what I said and everything— (*She lowers her voice guardedly, so as not to bring* BRIAN *in.*)

JIM. Yes. Look, I must go!

(*He goes out. She follows him.*)

AMY (*offstage*). 'Bye, Jimbo.

(*The outer door slams shut and, after a pause, she comes back. She leans against the inner door for a moment.*)

You should be very proud of your father, Brian, you know that?
(BRIAN *is eating a dish of cornflakes, shaking on sugar with a liberal hand.*)
BRIAN. I am. (*He picks up a newspaper, starts to read.*)
AMY. There aren't many men who would be big enough to apologize to their own sons.
BRIAN. I suppose not.
AMY (*moves down to table*). He's always been like that. If he's in the wrong, he's the first to admit it, and to apologize. Some people would call it weakness. In my opinion it shows great strength of character.
BRIAN. Mmm—
(AMY *moves down to fireplace.*)
AMY. Your father is a fine man—I hope you realize that fact. For instance, the way he's always found time for his family. Do you know the reason why he hasn't been more successful in business? Simply and solely because he refused to devote his entire life to his work, like some men. He refused to neglect his family.
BRIAN. Yes.
AMY. When you were a baby he would spend hour after hour playing with you, telling you stories, taking you out—to the Zoo, to the park, to the river. You used to spend hours by the river, watching the ships come and go. No matter how pressed he was, or how tired, you always came first. He always put you first. Brian—are you listening?
BRIAN. Uh-huh.
AMY. What was I saying then? (*She crosses U.S. of table and snatches paper from him.*)
BRIAN. Eh? Oh. Something about Dad?
AMY (*smiling*). Something about Dad! I bet you never heard a word I said! Never mind. In the years to come I hope you'll remember what a fine father you've had.
BRIAN. You make it sound as if he was leaving for an unknown land.
AMY (*quickly*). No. No—I didn't mean that. But children do forget quickly. It's easy to forget. You have a thousand—a million things to thank your father for, Brian, you know that?
(BRIAN *glances at her, curious at her intense manner. She goes* D.S. *to armchair and sits.*)
BRIAN. Mum, he's not dead, you know. There's a lot of life in the old dog yet!
AMY. Don't say things like that!
BRIAN. Well, you were talking as if we'd just got back from his funeral. Everything in the past tense.

AMY (*desperately*). I want you to appreciate your father! I want you to be grateful for all he has done, for all the sacrifices he has made! I don't want you to take it all for granted!

BRIAN (*puzzled*). Mum, I said I was proud of him. What do you want me to do—rig up a neon sign saying "Brian Preston thanks his father"? (*He crosses to her.*) Anyway, what about you? Haven't you done anything for me, then?

AMY (*passionately*). I've done nothing! Compared to your father I've done nothing!

(*He glances at her, then kneels in front of her.*)

BRIAN (*gently*). Mum—listen to me—what's eating you?

AMY. Nothing, nothing.

(*She tries to shake him off, but he holds her firmly.*)

BRIAN. You two have been fighting! I thought so last night. I could see it in your face.

AMY. No. It isn't that. Brian, I can talk to you—you're old enough to understand. Your father isn't happy.

BRIAN. He's just got a touch of the temporary blues, Mum. It's a mood. It'll pass.

AMY. This is more serious. I mean—how can I explain—he feels—he feels as though he's not getting anywhere, as if he's in a rut, do you see? I suppose a man gets like that sometimes. I mean, you're growing up—you don't need him so much—and he wonders what it's all been for—if it was worth it, you know?

BRIAN. It's not hard to understand, Mum. He is over forty. We must expect him to be a bit difficult sometimes. We'll just have to be diplomatic and try and cheer him up. You, too! You got to cheer up, too. I can't carry both of you. Come here. (*He gets up and pulls her up from the armchair. He kisses her.*) You know, I can still kiss you without embarrassment.

AMY. Thank you!

BRIAN. No, I didn't mean it that way. I mean—well, you know what they say in the books. They reckon all young people go through a phase when they despise their parents and hate the adult world. Well, the adult world gives me the dead needle at times, but so far I don't feel any hatred for my parents coming on. (*Lightly, but sincerely.*) Maybe I'm not normal. I'm grateful, I appreciate you and —not to get too mushy—I suppose I love you. Does that help?

AMY (*moved*). Oh, Brian.

(*She breaks away, goes into the kitchen quickly. He grins, shrugs, goes back to chair at table L. to his cornflakes, then starts up as he notices the time.*)

BRIAN. Cripes! Hey, Mum—

(AMY *comes back.* He gets up, crosses U.S.R. *to pick up school books.* AMY *is* U.S. *of table.*)
Look at the time. I've got to run—I'll be late!

AMY. Oh, Brian! I was going to get you bacon and eggs.

BRIAN. Now she tells me!

AMY. It won't take a minute. You ought to have something cooked. It's important for a growing boy to have plenty of protein.

BRIAN. Listen, don't call me a growing boy!

AMY. What are you, then? Anyway, you need protein. A protein deficiency can be very serious.

(BRIAN *crosses down to her.*)

BRIAN (*teasing*). How do you know?

AMY. Eh?

BRIAN. How do you know that a protein deficiency is serious?

AMY. Everybody knows that. It's universal knowledge. Anyway, I read all about it in "Reader's Digest".

BRIAN. Some time you should try reading a whole original book. I mean it. All this potted science and condensed literature—that can give you a real protein deficiency—did you know that? (*Taps his forehead.*) Up here. (*Kisses her.*) 'Bye. (*He moves to the door.*)

AMY. Brian, wait. What time will you be home this evening?

BRIAN. Round about six o'clock—usual time. But I'll be going straight out again. Taking Christine to the Film Society.

AMY. I'll have tea ready for you.

BRIAN. Fine.

(*As he moves off, she stops him again. She is embarrassed.*)

AMY. Brian!

BRIAN. Mum, I'll be late.

AMY. Brian, have you any money?

BRIAN. Me? Are you kidding!

AMY. That two pounds your aunt sent for your birthday, I wondered if— I'll pay you back, you know that. (*She crosses* D.S. *to mirror above fireplace.*)

BRIAN. I'm saving that money towards the school trip, Mum, I told you.

AMY. You won't need it for at least a month. I will pay you back, Brian.

BRIAN. What do you want it for?

AMY. I—I want to get my hair done—buy one or two things. I've got a little money—I need more.

BRIAN. Why this sudden concern over your looks? I mean, you don't usually go for that sort of jazz. Why start now?

AMY (*quietly*). All right. It doesn't matter. I'll manage.

(*He looks at her, purses his lips.*)

BRIAN. O.K. (*Smiles.*) I'll take a chance.

AMY. Oh, thanks, Brian. I will pay you back—honestly.

BRIAN. You'd better. (*Shakes his head.*) All of a sudden she wants to get her hair done— I'll get the money.

(*He hurries off to his room.* AMY *takes a tin from the shelf, rattles it, shakes out a few coins. She is obviously disappointed at the amount. She gets out her purse and brings out a little more money.*)

AMY (*counting*). Ten—eleven—twelve shillings—and sixpence. Two pounds from Brian—two pounds, twelve and six—not enough.

(*She looks around, desperately trying to think where she can lay her hands on more money. Her eye falls on her ring. She starts to take it off. It won't come. She crosses* U.S. *of table and takes some butter from the dish, and smears it on her finger. She starts to work the ring off.* BRIAN *comes back and she thrusts her hand behind her back. He comes down to* R. *of table.*)

BRIAN. What are you doing?

AMY. Nothing.

BRIAN. There's a strange air of mystery about this place today.

AMY. You're imagining things.

BRIAN. Oh no. There's something in the wind. The place is sort of subdued—quiet. (*Clicks his fingers.*) Cripes, I just realized—

AMY. What?

BRIAN. You haven't had the radio on once this morning. Not once. That's what's so strange—the silence!

AMY (*smiling in relief*). One day you'll get too clever, young feller-me-lad.

BRIAN. Here's your two pounds. I mean my two pounds. It's a loan, mind. This is strictly business.

(*She keeps her left hand behind her back, takes the notes with the other.*)

AMY. It's in a good cause—you'll see.

BRIAN. O.K. 'Bye, glamour-puss—

AMY. 'Bye, dear. (*Mechanically.*) Mind how you go. .

(*Exit* BRIAN. *She starts to work on the wedding ring once more. At last it comes off. She holds it up to the light, smiles in triumph.*)

It's in a good cause!

The lights fade.

CURTAIN

SCENE 2

Before curtain rises we hear sound of heavy rain and thunder.
Lights fade in on the PRESTON *living-room. After a moment or so,*
AMY *comes in. She drops shopping-bag on to armchair, kicks off her*
shoes, rushes to mirror, and with horror peels off the soaking wet silk
square which covers her hair.

She has obviously been walking through very heavy rain and is
wet through. Her hair is dripping and bedraggled, the work of the hair-
dresser wasted. The rain may still be heard, beating down, but the
thunder is growing fainter.

She groans. She takes off her wet coat, lets it fall to the floor.
She looks at her hair again, tries to pat it into shape.

She panics. She picks up coat, rushes into the kitchen, comes back with
a towel. She pats and dabs at her hair with this, standing in front of mirror.

She examines the result and is almost in tears as she cries:

AMY. It's no use. (*She takes a grip of herself, as a shiver goes through her.*)
Better let it dry. It'll be all right when it's dry.

(*She wraps the towel around her head, turban fashion. She puts*
her fingers to her lips in the characteristic gesture she makes when she is
trying to marshal her thoughts. She goes to her shopping-bag, gets out
a bottle of whisky she has bought for this evening. She shivers a little.
She looks round as though she is about to perform a guilty act. Then
she opens the bottle, takes a cup from sideboard U.S., *pours a little whisky*
into cup, and closing her eyes, as though taking medicine, she drains the
cup. She obviously doesn't like the taste and rubs her mouth, screws up
her face. She puts the cup down—suddenly clicks her fingers.)
The dress!

(*Hanging on the half-open door to the bedroom there is a dress—*
AMY'S *best dress. She hurries across, takes it down, smoothes it with*
her fingers. She puts it across chair R. *of table and slips out of her blouse*
and skirt, which she drops to the floor.

She starts to put on the dress. It won't go at first. She pauses,
breathing heavily, and takes off the towel. She glances at her hair in the
mirror, frowns. She has another go with the dress. It goes on over her
head, but she has difficulty in pulling it down over her hips. She pulls
and struggles, growing more desperate. She stops for breath, almost in
tears. Then she tries again, urging herself to be calm.)
Now—take it easy! Be careful—now—

(*But the injunction is wasted. The dress won't go on. It is far too*
tight. And as she pulls and tugs at it, the material gives way and splits.
The dress is ruined.)
Oh—no—no!

(*She begins to sob helplessly.* *Then this turns to savage anger and she claws at the dress, ripping it from her body.* HILDA *enters and watches in amazement from the door.*)

HILDA. Amy!

(AMY *looks up.*)

AMY. Go away—go away. Leave me alone.

(*She collapses in chair* R. *of table, sobbing, defeated.* HILDA *closes the door, comes forward quietly. She kneels beside the chair.*)

HILDA. Amy! Amy, love, what is it? What's wrong?

AMY. Everything—everything!

HILDA. Tell me. Come on, love. Do you good to talk. Tell me.

(*She gives* AMY *a handkerchief.* AMY *takes it, dabs her eyes, blows her nose.*)

AMY. I wanted to look nice. I had it all planned. I was going to be so cool—and—and—get the place looking neat and get drinks and everything. I wanted to show them I could do it.

HILDA. Why? What's it all about?

AMY. I told you—I wanted to have everything perfect. I even had my hair done. I haven't been to a hairdresser for ages. At first they were too busy to take me, but I begged the woman. I told her it was a very special occasion. She said I had attractive hair, but I'd neglected it. It's true—my hair used to be my best feature, but I've neglected it. It used to be my best feature—honestly.

(HILDA *lets her pour this out, then intervenes gently.*)

HILDA. Why was it so important today? (*She moves away,* U.S. *slightly.*)

AMY. Because—because— (*She checks herself.*) I just wanted to surprise Jimbo, that's all.

HILDA. That's all?

AMY. Yes, I wanted to surprise him. When they'd done my hair it looked so nice—honestly—it looked wonderful. Even the hairdresser said so! And I started to walk home, feeling wonderful. The sky was blue, Hilda, the sun was shining. I felt like a young girl. Then, suddenly, the rain! Did you hear that rain? The whole sky suddenly opened up!

HILDA. It's stopped now.

AMY. Yes—now! Look at my hair—just look—soaked, ruined. Ruined! It's worse than it was before.

HILDA. It's not that bad. I'll help you with it, and you've got another dress.

AMY. Nothing like this—nothing like this. Do you know what I paid for that dress? Four pounds—and that was five years ago when a pound really was a pound.

HILDA. If you've had it five years, you can't complain. You've had value for your money.

AMY. But I was relying on it! Today of all days it has to let me down.

HILDA. What makes tonight so important? I mean, is it that special?

AMY (*holding out her left hand*). Look!

HILDA. I don't see—(*Suddenly.*) Your ring—your wedding ring—where is it?

AMY (*solemnly*). I hocked it! Yes, I did. I pawned it for three pounds. That ring has never left my finger since the day Jimbo put it there. Not till today. It's a strange thing—just a ring—but without it I feel naked. (*She shivers a little, suddenly thrusts her left hand out of sight.*)

HILDA. Where's your dressing-gown?

AMY. In the bedroom.

(HILDA *goes into the bedroom.* AMY *rises and removes the remains of the dress from her body, holds a piece of it against her face.* HILDA *returns with the dressing-gown and helps her into it.*)

HILDA. Slip this on for a minute, while we work something out.

AMY. It was all for nothing. That's the awful thing. (*Almost breaking down again.*) Hilda—Hilda—I don't know what to do. I'm at my wits' end. I don't know which way to turn. Someone's got to help me—someone will have to help me.

HILDA (*gently*). I can't help unless you tell me what it's all about, Amy. I can't, can I?

AMY. Perhaps it's a punishment. It could be a punishment, Hilda. I haven't been inside a church or a chapel for years. I haven't—

HILDA. Oh, don't talk daft! Tell me what happened.

AMY. You wouldn't believe me.

HILDA. You've had a bull-and-a-cow with Jim—that it?

AMY. No, no! We've never had a row in the whole of our married life. (*A little pause, then, in a near whisper.*) He wants to leave me. He wants a divorce.

HILDA. Jim?

(AMY *nods.*)

Another woman?

(AMY *nods.*)

When did he tell you all this?

AMY. Last night.

HILDA. And all this—this business today—your hair and everything—you did all this because of him?

AMY. Yes.

HILDA. Well, now I've seen everything! I've been bang through the Elephant! I hand it to you, love, I really hand it to you. (*She moves above* AMY, U.S. *of table, and picks up the whisky.*) Who's been drinking?

W.D.G.–D

AMY. I have, just a little. I thought it might pick me up—I felt so chilled.

HILDA. A good idea! We'll have some more.

AMY. No—no. That's for Jimbo. I bought it for Jimbo.

HILDA. What he never has, he'll never miss. (*She takes another cup from top of sideboard and pours out two whiskies. She holds a cup out for* AMY.) Here, put this where the buses can't run over it.

AMY. It's for Jimbo, Hilda.

HILDA. And he deserves it? Drink!

AMY (*taking the cup*). It's horrible. I don't like it.

HILDA. Drink.

(*The first whisky is beginning to affect* AMY. *She smiles suddenly, laughs a little hysterically.*)

AMY. Why not!

(HILDA *drains her cup.* AMY *sips at hers.*)

HILDA. Come on—put it down!

(AMY *drains her cup.*)

That's better, eh?

AMY. Ugh. I don't know how people can drink this stuff.

(HILDA *splashes some more whisky into the cups.*)

HILDA. My mother had the right ideas, you know. She said the Government ought to shoot twelve men every Friday.

AMY. Why Friday?

HILDA. Why not?

(*They both laugh.*)

I nods me head, I catches your eye—and down the little red lane!

AMY. Cheers.

(*They drink again.*)

HILDA. This'll put the curl back into your hair, love.

AMY. Do I look a mess?

(AMY *sits* R. *of table.* HILDA *sits* C. *of table.*)

HILDA. No, I wouldn't say that. You look as if you'd been pulled through a hedge backwards—otherwise you're all right.

(*They both laugh.* HILDA *pours some more whisky.*)

Well, who's the girl he's stuck on, someone in the office?

AMY. The boss's secretary.

HILDA. Oi-yoi! I knew it. These secretaries—there ought to be a law! All they've got is one idea—and it's got nothing to do with shorthand.

AMY. I thought you were a secretary once.

HILDA. I was. That's how I know.

(*They both giggle at this. They sip their whiskies.*)

Mind you, the men are just as bad. I mean—the way they look at you. Every time you walk through the office you can feel their hot little eyes burning your legs. (*She drinks.*) All men are bastards. And the married ones are super-bastards with trimmings. Men run the world for their own benefit.

AMY. I never worked in an office. I worked in a shop. Some of the assistants there were a bit hard to handle. Always touching you for no reason—sort of pretending to brush past and touching you.

HILDA. They're the worst, the maulers. You know the answer, don't you?

AMY. What?

HILDA. Bring your knee up. Wonderful how that seems to quieten 'em down.

(*She demonstrates this defensive action. They laugh again.* HILDA *pours some more whisky, spilling some.* AMY *starts to sing "Oh, Oh, Antonio", gently to herself.* HILDA *looks at her, cuts in quickly.*)

Did I tell you about the time the Assistant Sales Manager asked me to work late? Nice-looking feller, really—a bit on the fleshy side, but tall with it—you know. Anyway, while I'm typing the stuff back in the typists' room, he starts hitting the bottle. Then he comes out to me and starts talking about the creative instinct.

AMY (*laughing*). The—

HILDA. That's what the man said. The creative instinct. And a lot of bull-shine about prime—prime—about the primeval urge.

AMY. What's that, for heaven's sake?

HILDA. Whatever it is, it's dirty. This was his line, you see. Well, he's getting real sticky, breathing down my neck, telling me I got nice skin.

AMY. You have. I always admired your complexion.

(*They put their faces close together.*)

HILDA. Not like it used to be. I mean it used to be really something —not a blemish, you know what I mean? Where was I? Oh, this feller. Well, when he starts telling me about Adam and Eve, I thought it was time for action. I played silly beggars with him around the desk for a few minutes, just to tire him out, and then I pushed the typewriter off my desk. It fell on his foot and broke three of his toes. Last I saw of the Assistant Sales Manager he was in an ambulance.

(AMY *suddenly starts to sing.*)

AMY. "The rain in Spain stays mainly on the plain."

HILDA (*looks at her astonished for a moment, then joins in*). "The rain in Spain stays mainly on the plain."

(*They sing a few bars of the song and beat out rhythms on the table.*)

AMY. That was a wonderful show.

HILDA. Didn't see it.

AMY. We went one Christmas—no, just before Christmas. Let's have some more whisky.

HILDA. There isn't much left.

(*She pours some more.* AMY *starts to roar with laughter.*)
What are you laughing at? What's funny? Come on, let me share the joke. Come on—tell Hilda!

AMY. The—the creative instinct!

HILDA (*laughing*). Yes! That's what he actually said. The crea—creative instinct. He said he had a highly developed creative instinct.

AMY (*deliberately, and quite quietly*). All men are bastards.

HILDA. Let's drink to that!

(*They stand up, raise their cups, drink.* HILDA *drains the bottle into the cups.*)
It's finished. Mmm—you should have bought a bigger bottle. (*Reads drunkenly from the label.*) "Highest Awards—Sydney 1880, Brisbane 1897—Paris 1885—"

AMY (*suddenly*). I want to go to Paris.

HILDA. We'll both go! (*She clasps* AMY *and they embrace.*) Leave everything and go to Paris!

AMY. We'll go round the world!

HILDA. Why not? The whole world! And after that, we'll go to the moon. No—wouldn't like that—not the moon.

AMY. Definitely not the moon.

HILDA. We'll stick to the earth.

AMY. Drink to that.

(*They drain their cups.* AMY *giggles, raises her cup.*)
Wait! Hilda—watch!

(*She tries to click her heels Prussian fashion, then throws her cup against the kitchen door.* HILDA *laughs in delight and does the same with her cup.*)
Saw them do that in a picture once. Ronald Colman was in it. Only they had glasses.

HILDA. Should have glasses.

AMY. I got some glasses. (*She sways across* U.S.R. *to get the glasses.*)

HILDA. Never mind—no more whisky.

AMY. No more whisky. (*She comes back* C.) Hilda, tell you what. When we go to Paris—we go on our own. Absolutely alone. All on our own-e-oh! No Jimbo—no Willie.

HILDA. Oh no! I must have Willie.

AMY. What do you mean, you must have Willie?

HILDA. I must have Willie. That's what I mean.

AMY. Why?

HILDA. Why what?

AMY. Why must you—whatever you said.

HILDA. Exactly. Must take Willie.

AMY. You don't want Willie!

HILDA (*aggrieved*). Don't you tell me I don't want Willie. If Willie can't come, then neither can I.

AMY. You want Willie? You actually want him?

HILDA. Naturally I want him! I love Willie! Not many men study and work like he does, let me tell you. Besides, he knows his onions. He knows what's what.

AMY. You told me—you told me he wouldn't look at you—that's what you told me. You told me you took all your clothes off and he wouldn't look at you.

HILDA. What!

AMY. That's what you said.

HILDA. What did I say?

AMY. You took all your clothes off.

HILDA. When?

AMY. What do you mean—when?

HILDA. When did I—what did you say?

AMY. I don't remember.

(*There is a pause while they both try to focus their thoughts.*)

HILDA. Did I say I took my clothes off?

AMY. Yes—that was it.

HILDA. All of them?

AMY. That's what you said.

HILDA. When?

AMY. What do you mean—when?

HILDA. For heaven's sake! When?

AMY. I don't know.

HILDA. You don't know.

AMY. I don't know.

HILDA (*triumphantly*). You see? I'm surprised at you listening to such talk! I thought you were my friend, Amy. I shall know better in future.

AMY. You didn't take your clothes off?

HILDA (*with dignity*). What do you take me for? If you must know, I kept my knickers on.

AMY. I suppose that makes all the difference.

HILDA. It certainly does! Most certainly does!

AMY. Makes all the difference! (*She goes to table, picks up the bottle and turns it upside down.*)

Empty!

(HILDA *takes bottle and drops it on the floor*, D.S.L. *of table.*)

HILDA. Dead soldier.

(AMY *suddenly starts singing again and* HILDA *joins her.*)

AMY. "Oh, oh, Antonio—he's gone away,
   Left me all alone-e-oh, all on my own-e-oh—
BOTH. I'd like to meet him with his new sweetheart,
   Then up would go Antonio and his ice-cream cart!"
      (*They laugh and go into a dance round the table, singing the words.
   AMY leads way round armchair R. and HILDA jumps on to armchair,
   standing up uncertainly. AMY finishes D.S.R. of armchair. HILDA
   conducts the last of the singing, which they try to harmonize. As they
   finish, laughing, WILLIE enters, goes down to L. of armchair. HILDA
   swings round.*)
WILLIE. Hilda!
HILDA. Huh? Go away!
WILLIE. Hilda! You're drunk!
HILDA (*with dignity*). Drunk! That's an insult! (*She aims a slap at his
   face, but misses, almost losing her balance.*)
WILLIE. Do you want me to carry you out?
      (HILDA *throws her arms round him affectionately.* AMY *is sitting
   on stool* D.S.R.)
HILDA. Oh yes! Carry me. Willie, carry me. Carry me to bed like
   you used to on Sunday afternoons.
WILLIE (*scandalized*). Hilda—pull yourself together!
HILDA. You know what, sweetheart? You got no creative instinct.
   A man's gotta have a creative instinct. Gotta have a prime—prime—
   gotta have an evil instinct. Kiss me! I'm your wife—kiss me! (*She
   falls across his shoulder.*)
WILLIE. I'm taking you out of here!
      (*He marches out, half-carrying her.* HILDA *squeals with delight.*)
HILDA. 'Bye, Amy! Going to bed now. Going to bed with Willie—
      (AMY *gives her a feeble wave. The door crashes behind* WILLIE
   and HILDA. AMY *is running down now.*)
AMY (*singing in subdued tones*). "Left me all alone-e-oh, all on my
   own-e-oh, I'd like to meet him with his new sweetheart—"
      (*She tries to pull herself together and gets up from stool.*)
Jimbo! What's the time?
      (*She sways over to the clock on mantelshelf, puts her face close to
   it in an effort to read the time.*)
Jimbo!
      (*She starts to prepare the table. She clears it off first, by dumping
   whatever is there on chairs. She pauses, thinking. Then she goes to the
   cupboard, opens the door. A pile of things cascade out on to the floor.
   She rummages inside desperately, comes out with a table covering. She
   hauls herself up, spreads the cloth with difficulty over the table.*)

She takes a trayful of crockery and cutlery from sideboard and starts to set places.)
Jimbo here—Georgie opposite. Georgie! No—why should she eat with us!
(She throws the knife and fork intended for GEORGIE *on to the floor,* D.S.L. *of table.)*
No—she's got to eat. Got to be civilized—got to talk about it—
(She kneels to recover the knife and fork. She finds the empty whisky bottle on the floor where it has been dropped by HILDA.*)*
All gone, Jimbo's whisky—all gone.
(She peers at the label.)
Red Label! Old Scotch Whisky.
(She turns the bottle upside down.)
All gone—poor Jimbo—it's all gone. *(Reads the label.)* "By appointment to Her Majesty the Queen".
(She giggles, starts to sing.)
"Oh, oh, Antonio—he's gone away,
Left me all alone-e-oh—-
Her voice tails off. She tries to get up, clutches the table cover and pulls it down, bringing down also a great clutter of crockery and cutlery She sinks to the floor, D.S. *in front of table, and closes her eyes. She sings a little more of the song, then her voice fades away.*

(BLACKOUT.)

After a pause to show passage of one hour, lights fade in.
BRIAN *enters. He is whistling cheerily. He breaks off, appalled by the chaos in the room, hurries to his mother. He picks up the bottle, frowns.*
BRIAN. Mum—Mum!
(He raises her head and shoulders. She opens her eyes, smiles giddily.)
AMY. Brian—
BRIAN. What happened, Mum? What have you been doing?
AMY. Whisky all gone. Leave me alone—want to sleep; I'm tired—want to sleep.
BRIAN. Come on. Here—come on. You'd better lie down.
AMY. That's right—lie down—let me lie down—
BRIAN. Not here. In your bedroom. Come on, I'll help you.
(He helps her up. She sways, clings to him.)
It's O.K. You'll be O.K. I've got you. *(He starts to move towards the bedroom.)*
AMY *(in anguish)*. I won't let you do it, Jimbo. I won't let you do it—I won't—I won't— I won't let you do it.

(*He keeps her moving. They go into the bedroom. We can still hear her voice.*)
I won't let you do it, Jimbo—I won't—I won't—I won't—
(*Her voice tails away.*)
BRIAN (*offstage*). There you are. You'll be all right. You lie there—you'll be O.K. now.
(*He comes out of the bedroom.* JIM *enters, looks round the room in horror.*)
JIM (*quickly*). Brian—what's wrong?
BRIAN. Something's—I don't know—Mum is—
JIM (*cutting in, alarmed*). She's not—she's not done anything to herself?
BRIAN. No. I think—I think she's drunk.
(JIM *moves to the bedroom door. Then he remembers* GEORGIE. *He turns to the front door.*)
JIM. Georgie—
(*She steps forward.* BRIAN *looks at her, puzzled.*)
Amy is sick.
GEORGIE. Maybe I'd better go.
JIM. No. Not yet, anyway. Come in. Oh, Brian—you've heard me speak of Miss Barlow—Georgie— This is Brian, Georgie.
BRIAN. Hi.
GEORGIE. Hello.
JIM. I'll just see how she is.
(*He goes into the bedroom. There is an awkwardness between the others.* BRIAN *crosses* D.S. *of table, starts to clear up the debris, putting it on tray.*)
GEORGIE. Let me help you.
BRIAN. Thanks.
(*She goes* D.S.R. *of* BRIAN. *They work in silence for a moment or two. There is an awkwardness between them.*)
GEORGIE. Preston—I mean your father—has talked about you so much I feel I know you.
BRIAN. Yeh.
GEORGIE. He tells me you like trad jazz.
BRIAN. Some.
GEORGIE. I can take it—in small doses. Not too much at a time.
(*She is trying to get on terms, but not too obviously. He is wary. He doesn't answer.*)
Your father is a great fan of Duke Ellington, I believe. So he tells me, anyway.
BRIAN. Yeh.
(*He picks up bottle and rises from floor.* GEORGIE *puts tray on table.* JIM *comes back, closing the door quietly.*)

JIM. I think she's all right. She'll sleep. What happened, Brian? (*He goes* D.S. *to* L. *of armchair.*)
BRIAN. You know as much as I do. I just got back. I found the room like this. And she was lying on the floor.
JIM. I don't understand. She hardly ever drinks.
(BRIAN *tosses the bottle to his father, and* JIM *catches it.* GEORGIE *is now* U.S. *between them.*)
BRIAN. Today she did. Take a look for yourself. A whole flask of whisky. What made her do that?
(JIM *glances quickly at* GEORGIE *and then away again.*)
GEORGIE. Perhaps I'd better make myself useful. Would you like some coffee, Brian?
(*He ignores her—his eyes on* JIM.)
(*Quickly.*) I dare say we could all do with some coffee. The kitchen is through here, isn't it? (*She goes through to the kitchen, taking tray with her.*)
BRIAN (*lowering his voice*). What is she doing here?
JIM. I brought her back to meet your mother.
BRIAN. Why?
JIM. To meet your mother. She's been here before—well—she's been here a couple of times.
(BRIAN *crossses to* JIM.)
BRIAN. Dad, I wasn't born yesterday. What's going on? Why should Mum get drunk? What's going on?
JIM. Nothing for you to worry your head over.
BRIAN (*tense*). Dad—don't speak to me as if I were a six-year-old child or something. I live in this house. Whatever's going on, I've got a right to know!
JIM (*with rising anger*). I said—nothing that concerns you!
BRIAN (*sarcastic*). That's a good lyric—put a tune to it and sing it!
JIM. Now listen. I warned you this morning—I'm warning you again! Watch your tongue! You were damn rude to Georgie just now—
BRIAN. What's she doing here? (*He pauses, glances towards kitchen, then back to* JIM.) Are you walking out on Mum?
JIM. I'm not walking out on anyone, as you put it.
BRIAN. You're leaving her?
JIM. Nothing's settled, nothing's fixed.
BRIAN. But you want to. You're planning to leave—
JIM. Brian, you don't understand—
BRIAN. What is there to understand? It's as plain as daylight. You've found yourself a young popsy, and you're ditching us. Charming—charming!
JIM. Brian!

W.D.G.–E

BRIAN. And this morning you had the brass to tell me—tell me—to have more respect for my mother. You—and that—that scrubber!
(*JIM hits BRIAN across the face, hard. BRIAN stares at him, white-faced. Then he moves U.S. to door C.*)

JIM. Brian—where are you going?

BRIAN. Don't worry—I'll be back. I'm not walking out on her. (*He opens the door, turns back to his father. His stammering is quite painful now.*) Don't ever hit me again, Dad. Don't you ever lay a finger on me again.

(*He goes out. The door slams. JIM looks up, sees GEORGIE standing in the doorway to the kitchen.*)

GEORGIE. I'd better go.

JIM. No, no. Stay—please. (*He sits wearily in armchair.*) Please.

GEORGIE (*after a little pause*). He's a nice-looking boy.

JIM. I never raised a hand to him before—not once. And Amy—she never touched spirits—I've never known her to look at spirits.

GEORGIE. You're tearing up roots. You can't expect it to be painless. There's no anaesthetic for this, darling.

JIM. There ought to be some way to be happy without having to trample on other people. It ought to be possible.

GEORGIE. It ought to be, but it isn't.

JIM. When I first came in, I was scared—I was scared she'd done something to herself. She could do that, you know—she's capable of doing anything.

GEORGIE. She won't.

JIM. You're always so sure, always so dead sure.
(*She goes down to L. of armchair.*)

GEORGIE (*quietly*). Someone has to be, Preston.

JIM. How do you know you're right about me? How do you know? Perhaps I'm in my natural place after all—just a little man who's gone about as far as he can go.

GEORGIE. Preston, please. Look, I'm going to say this again, just once. Never mind about me, think of yourself. You've got to make a break for your own sake; if you draw back now it's this, or Simpson, for the rest of your life. I know it's hard, but don't draw back now.

JIM (*nodding, sadly*). All right. I'll be all right, Georgie. (*With a wry smile.*) We should have met twenty years ago.

GEORGIE. It wouldn't have helped. I was three at the time. (*She gives him a light kiss.*) I'll get the coffee.

(*She moves into the kitchen. JIM rises, lights a cigarette, then busies himself wearily with picking up the remainder of the debris. He moves D.S.L. of table.*
The click of a lock makes him spin round. AMY enters. She is

wearing the old dressing-gown, and looks like death. But there is a certain determination about the set of her mouth.)

JIM. Amy! You shouldn't be up.

AMY *(wearily).* I'm better on my feet.

JIM. You ought to be in your bed.

AMY. I'll be all right. *(She looks towards kitchen as she hears rattle of cups.)*

JIM. Georgie is making some coffee.

AMY. Georgie? Oh yes—Georgie. *(She moves down to fireplace, checks herself in mirror.)*

JIM. Would you like some aspirin or something?

AMY. No. Have you got a handkerchief?

> *(He goes to her and hands her one. She blows her nose, screwing up her forehead with the pain it brings to her head.)*

JIM. You look all in. You ought to be in bed.

> *(She pats her hair, lets her hand drop hopelessly.)*

AMY. I was going to surprise you. I had my hair done special—and I was going to put on my best dress. I got the place looking so neat and clean. I was going to surprise you. I even bought some brandy— I mean—whisky. I planned it so we could talk together, the three of us, like civilized people. And it all went wrong, everything went wrong.

JIM. It doesn't matter, Amy.

AMY. That dress—it wouldn't fit any more, Jimbo, I mean—it just wouldn't fit. And after they did my hair I got caught in the rain. I wish you could have seen my hair.

JIM. It doesn't matter.

AMY *(with a flash of passion).* It matters to me, Jimbo! It matters to me! *(The passion dies.)* No—it doesn't matter. I suppose it isn't really important, after all.

> *(GEORGIE comes in, bearing a tray with coffee-pot, etc. She puts this on table. AMY crosses U.S. to her.)*

Oh, you shouldn't be doing that—in my house—let me—

GEORGIE. It's no trouble, Mrs. Preston.

AMY. But I should— *(Falling back.)* Thanks, anyway. It's good of you.

GEORGIE. Milk?

AMY. No. No, thank you. I'd better have it black, no sugar.

> *(GEORGIE hands her a cup of coffee.)*

GEORGIE. There we are.

AMY. Thank you. *(Sips coffee.)* Very nice.

> *(GEORGIE hands JIM a cup, which she has sugared, crossing behind AMY, so that she is now U.S.C.)*

Won't you have a cup?

GEORGIE. No, I won't, thanks. I must go—I have things to do.

AMY. But we were going to talk! I thought that was the whole idea.

GEORGIE. Don't you think it would be better if we discussed—if we talked it over some other evening?

AMY. No! No, I want to discuss it now—tonight!

(GEORGIE *glances at* JIM.)

JIM. It might be better to leave it for a while, Amy.

AMY (*flashing again*). No! I can't. I can't wait, Jimbo. I have to know, don't you understand, I have to know.

(JIM *motions* GEORGIE *to chair* R. *of table.* AMY *sits* C. *and sips her coffee.* JIM *stands just behind* GEORGIE.)

I was telling Jimbo. I planned it all to be so different. I had this evening all planned. I'm sorry.

GEORGIE. It doesn't matter.

AMY. That's what he said. (*She puts down her cup, waits expectantly.*)

JIM (*awkwardly*). Well—

AMY. Yes, Jimbo?

JIM. Well—as I said, Amy—

AMY. As you said. You want a divorce so that you can marry Georgie.

JIM. Yes.

AMY. And that's all you have to say?

JIM. No. Not all. But—well—that's the main thing.

AMY. Yes. I suppose when you think about it there isn't much to add to that. I mean, what can you say? It takes twenty years to build a home and you can break it up in twenty minutes. That's the truth whichever way you look at it.

GEORGIE. Mrs. Preston—we didn't ask this to happen.

AMY (*bitterly*). You didn't ask, but it happened. You could have said he's someone else's husband, you could have said he belongs to someone else, you could have got out of that office and left him alone—but you didn't. (*She gets up, turns back* C., *facing sideboard.*)

JIM. Amy, we won't get anywhere if you talk like that.

GEORGIE. No, Preston, let her speak.

AMY (*turning in anger*). Oh yes—let her speak in her own house! The perfect secretary—so calm, so cool and efficient. Let her speak, she says!

JIM. Amy, this won't get us anywhere. You asked me to bring Georgie here to talk. We've been honest about it; we've been open about everything.

AMY (*as though she hadn't heard*). So calm and cool. And pretty, too. Nice legs, nice figure. I had a good figure once, you know. You find that hard to believe? I had a wonderful figure—right up until

our second baby was born. Did you know we had another child?
A girl—we called her June—she was born in June—
GEORGIE. Preston told me about her.
AMY (*fiercely*). Preston! Preston! His name is Jim! You're not
a schoolteacher calling the register. (*More quietly.*) We lost June.
That's a terrible thing when you think of it. She only lived half an
hour—she had thirty minutes of life in this world. That's when I
lost my figure—women do when they have children sometimes.
(*Harshly.*) You might lose your figure when you have children—
you know that?
JIM. Amy, Georgie and me—we've talked it over. If it's all right with
you, I'll move out at the week-end. That'll give us a few days to
settle up—well—the other matters, money and so forth.
AMY. I don't need any money from you, Jimbo.
JIM. You'll need something.
AMY. I don't need money from you! The week-end, you say? Why
wait until the week-end?
JIM. Well, we thought—
AMY. We thought! She thought, you mean. She's done all the
thinking. I've lived with you too long. I know you. You couldn't
have done this on your own.
GEORGIE (*calmly*). The week-end, then?
AMY. Of course, of course! It's all organized—all arranged—the
efficient secretary on the job. Just like borrowing a cup of sugar.
You walk into someone's house and you say, "Pardon me, but will it
be all right if I take your husband at the week-end? Will that be
convenient?" You're like a fish. I look at you and I see a fish—cold
—without feeling—
　　　(GEORGIE *turns away and moves* D.S. *of armchair.* AMY *goes to*
　　her.)
Don't turn your back to me. Don't you dare turn your back on me!
Look at me—look at me! (GEORGIE *turns to her.*) Or are you
ashamed? When I think—I was going on my knees to you! Yes,
I was! That's why I asked him to bring you here. I was going to
beg you to give him back to me. I had it all worked out. I was
even prepared to share him with you—I was going to offer to share
him—anything so long as he could stay here. I was going on my
knees to you!
GEORGIE. Mrs. Preston—please—
AMY. What does a woman like you want with a man like him? He's
not handsome or clever; he won't make any fortunes. He'll be old
in ten years. What made you pick on him?
GEORGIE (*sincerely*). I love him.

AMY. You love him! (*She laughs dryly, turns away* U.S., *then turns back.*) You want to sleep with him—that's what you want. Love—you don't know the meaning of the word. Do you know he snores? That he loses his temper if his newspaper is creased or folded the wrong way? That he can't stand sunshine and has to sit in the shade —that he gets rheumatism every winter and it's getting worse—that he smothers his food in tomato sauce—whatever it is—he smothers it in sauce? You know a thousand things about him—I know a million! That's what being married means! To know a million things about a person, to know a man inside out and still love him! Marriage isn't one long Sunday afternoon, you know—you've got to take the Monday mornings, too! (*She moves round armchair to fireplace.*)

GEORGIE (*after a pause, quietly*). Mrs. Preston, I came here tonight at your request. I came to talk this over, to explain.

AMY. All right. Talk. Explain. I'm listening—

GEORGIE. You're not making it very easy.

AMY. Good!

(GEORGIE *crosses* U.S.C. *to* JIM.)

GEORGIE. I tried to tell you—we neither of us asked this to happen.

AMY. But it did.

GEORGIE. Why did it happen? Why don't you ask yourself that question?

AMY. We were all right until you came along.

GEORGIE. No, Mrs. Preston. You can blame me if it gives you any satisfaction, but that's not the whole answer. I didn't go to that office looking for a lover. I wasn't panting for an affair with a married man. At first I hardly noticed him, and then one lunch-time we went into a café and he began to talk. The words seemed to pour out of him. He spoke about his dreams, his ambitions, all the things he had wanted to do with his life. (*She takes his hand.*) I wanted to cry. He spoke like an old man, you see, as though all that was past history. He's not old, he's still young, and yet he spoke as though his life had come to a standstill. You say you love him, you say you know him inside out—

AMY. It's the truth.

GEORGIE. Do you know anything about his work? He runs that firm, he runs Simpson's. Believe me, I know. I've seen it. Simpson is nothing. Jim is worth a dozen like him. Yet he stays there, he stays on—year after year—year after year. Well, he's worth more than that, don't you see? He could do so much more!

AMY. With you behind him, of course.

GEORGIE. Yes.

AMY. Of course. It all comes back to the same thing. You want him, you're determined to have him and you don't care who suffers in the process.

(GEORGIE *is beginning to crack now, and she turns to* JIM *for help.*)

GEORGIE. Preston, this is—I can't—I'd better go, I think.

JIM. No, Georgie, wait. Amy, for God's sake, be fair.

AMY. Be fair! You say that to me? Be fair?

JIM. Yes, I do! You talk as if there was only one side to this—this business. All right—I'm no angel with wings, I admit it. But God knows, I've tried to make something of our life. I tried. I've worked and sweated—for what? In twenty years of marriage what have we built, what have we achieved? We haven't even got a decent home, not even that.

AMY. But we've been happy, Jimbo. You can't deny that—we've been happy.

JIM. You've been happy, Amy—maybe you've been happy.

AMY. And you, too!

JIM (*shaking his head*). No. No, Amy. Perhaps years ago—not any more.

AMY (*bitterly*). Why didn't you tell me? You never even hinted you weren't happy—not once.

JIM. I didn't know, Amy, that's the reason. We did all right. We got a few laughs, we had Brian to think of. The days passed. We learned the trick of living together. We made a rut and settled in it. I suppose we could have gone on like that. Only I met Georgie, and I found out that I was firing on one cylinder. I found out I was only living half a life.

AMY. We were happy at the beginning. You loved me then.

JIM. Yes, of course.

AMY. Of course. While I was young—when I had my looks—I suited you.

JIM. Amy—

AMY. That's the truth.

JIM. It's not the whole truth. Amy, if you'd only admit—

AMY (*cutting in*). Admit that I've got faults? Jimbo, believe me, I'm very conscious of that. The list of my failings would stretch from here to the Chinese border. (*She sits on stool* D.S.R.) What are you looking for—perfection? Is she perfect then—no blemishes?

JIM. Of course not. That isn't the point.

AMY. Then what is the point, Jimbo? You want a young girl in your bed again, to remind you of your youth? You want love without responsibility?

JIM. Amy—I love Georgie. It's as simple as that.

AMY. You love Georgie now, and you don't love me any more. As simple as that.

JIM. I'm fond of you, Amy, you know that.

AMY (*bitterly*). Thank you. The staff are not allowed to accept gratuities.

GEORGIE. I'll go, Preston. There's nothing more I can say.

AMY (*rising*). Wait—he can go with you!

(GEORGIE *pauses, gives a little shrug, looks at* JIM.)

JIM. We've a few things to settle, Amy.

AMY. There's nothing to settle—I want you out of here tonight! The quicker, the better. Don't worry, I'll manage. I'm not going to sit back and weep. I don't need you, Jimbo. I can work, I can find a job. I've got Brian—we'll manage together. Maybe this is the best thing that could happen to me. For years I haven't thought of myself—only you. Now it's changed. (*To* GEORGIE.) Take him! He's all yours—take him—and get out of my home!

(*There is a little silence.*)

JIM. If that's what you want—

AMY. That's what I want!

JIM. I'm sorry.

AMY. Oh, don't be sorry. That's too soft and sentimental; it won't go down well with her. Don't be sorry—save your breath to cool your coffee.

(JIM *moves towards the bedroom.*)

JIM. I'll pack a few things.

(*He goes into the bedroom.* AMY *turns on* GEORGIE *fiercely.*)

AMY. And you—you—wait outside, wait downstairs—anywhere. You're not waiting here!

(GEORGIE *moves to the door.*)

GEORGIE. Will you let me say one word?

AMY. If you can think of one.

GEORGIE (*sincerely*). I just want to say—whatever you may think of me —I am truly sorry, I really am deeply sorry.

(*She has difficulty in speaking. She is so obviously sincere that* AMY *stares at her for a moment, and her bitterness seems to dissolve.*)

AMY. Yes. (*A pause, then gently.*) Sit down a minute. I didn't mean— Sit down.

(GEORGIE *sits in chair* R. *of table.* AMY *moves towards the bedroom.*)

I'd better help Jimbo. He never knows where to find anything. (*But she stops.*) I don't mean to be unkind. But when you saw what

was happening, couldn't you—somehow—I mean—couldn't you
have found the strength to leave him alone?
>   (GEORGIE *makes an ineffectual motion with her hands.* AMY *comes
>   down to her.*)
You're so pretty, you see—you're so attractive. You could have
anyone. You've got your whole life in front of you. Jimbo's not
for you—I'm not just saying that—I really mean it. I know him so
well, you see. He's weak, like me. We're peas out of the same pod;
we're a pair—well-matched—know what I mean?
>   (*She goes into the bedroom.* GEORGIE *sighs deeply. She looks
>   around the room, gets up. The door opens and* BRIAN *enters. There is
>   an edgy silence. He stands looking at her. She is near to breaking-point
>   now. He crosses to fireplace.*)
GEORGIE. You—you mustn't think too badly of your father.
BRIAN (*with contempt*). You make me sick!
GEORGIE (*desperate*). No—please—please—try to understand.
BRIAN. I'd like to understand! I'd like to understand what kind of
woman you are!
GEORGIE. People can't help their feelings!
BRIAN. Bring a gun next time! Kill her! It won't be so painful. You
make me sick!
>   (GEORGIE, *trembling, moves* U.S.C. *to the door.*)
GEORGIE. Tell your father I can't fight any— (*She breaks off, tries to
control herself.*) Tell him—just tell him—good-bye, God bless.
BRIAN. You're going?
GEORGIE. Yes.
BRIAN. Without him.
GEORGIE. Without him. (*She comes back a little, standing* U.S.C.) You're
young. You pray—you pray hard it never happens to you like this!
>   (*She speaks with great feeling, turns and goes out quickly. He
>   follows her, watches her go, then comes back slowly, thoughtfully.* AMY
>   *comes out of the bedroom, carrying a small case in her arms—it is not
>   fastened.* JIM *follows her.*)
AMY. This old case has seen better days, Jimbo. You ought to get a
new one.
>   (*She comes* D.S.C. *of table and puts case on table. She breaks off,
>   seeing that* GEORGIE *has gone.* JIM *stands* U.S.C.)
JIM. Where is she?
BRIAN. Gone.
JIM. What do you mean—gone? (*Angrily.*) What did you say to her?
BRIAN. She said to tell you—good-bye, God bless.
AMY. She can't have got very far, Jimbo. If you hurry, you'll catch
her.

JIM. Yes. (*He looks from Amy to* BRIAN.) Yes.

BRIAN (*an appeal*). Dad!

AMY (*quickly*). No, Brian, no!

   (JIM *hurries out.* AMY *turns* U.S. *to table, her back to audience.* BRIAN *goes to her.*)

BRIAN. Don't cry, Mum, don't cry.

AMY (*turning to him, with an effort*). I'll be all right. I'm past tears.

BRIAN. You're not to worry. I'll look after you. I'll always look after you.

   (*He takes her in his arms. She breaks suddenly.*)

AMY. His case! He forgot his case! (*She picks it up and it falls open, throwing the contents on the floor below table.*)

BRIAN. I'll pick it up.

AMY. No, I'll do it. Isn't that just like me? I'll do it. You make some tea.

   (*She kneels wearily, starts to repack the case.* BRIAN *goes into the kitchen.* JIM *comes back, moves slowly* D.S. *to* R. *of table.* AMY *is not aware of him until she sees his legs. She looks up.*)

I spilled your things.

   (*He nods. She puts case back on table, moves round* L. *of table, looking at him.*)

Didn't you catch her?

     (*He shakes his head.*)

But she couldn't have got very far.

JIM. I didn't try.

AMY. Jimbo—

   (*He looks at her helplessly, goes down and sits in armchair.*)

JIM. I'm a weak man—I'm no Simpson.

     (*She crosses to him.*)

AMY. Who wants a man like him, anyway? All those things I said—I didn't mean to hurt you, Jimbo. I wouldn't deliberately hurt you—

JIM. I know.

AMY. It'll be all right. It'll be all right from now on, I promise. I'll make a real effort.

JIM. Oh, Amy, don't talk like that!

AMY. But I mean it, Jimbo!

JIM. No, no. We have to face it, Amy—we'll never alter. We are what we are. You know, in a strange sort of way, I'm relieved it's over. She—she didn't know me, you see. I would have disappointed her—know what I mean? I was afraid of that all the time.

AMY. We're not old, Jimbo—we've still got time to be happy.

JIM. Yes. We've still got time—

(BRIAN *comes in with tea. He stops on seeing his father.* AMY *gestures to him to make no comment.*)

AMY. I'll get another cup.

(*She goes into the kitchen.* BRIAN *takes a cup to* JIM.)

BRIAN. Tea, Dad?

JIM (*taking it*). Thanks.

BRIAN. Dad, would you be very shocked if I told you I was on the verge of becoming an agnostic?

JIM. What?

BRIAN. You see, I've been thinking over this religious question. I've been giving it a lot of thought. And the plain fact is—I don't really know whether I believe in the existence of a God—you know? Here—I've got to take part in a sort of discussion at the club to-morrow—I drafted out a few notes. Would you like to look 'em over for me? (*He crosses to* JIM *with some notes.*) I'd like you to look at them, Dad.

JIM (*taking the notes*). All right, son.

(AMY *comes back.*)

AMY. Brian, I don't think you should bother your father with that stuff tonight.

JIM. It's all right. I don't mind.

AMY. What is it? Notes for another speech?

(*She stands at table watching them.* BRIAN *moves* U.S. *above armchair.* JIM *isn't reading the notes—he is looking ahead.*

Lights fade slowly, but they are still held in a spot of light.)

Know what? It's quiet in here—honestly, I just realized—

She crosses, switches on the radio, and is about to bang it, when she checks herself. She looks at JIM, *at* BRIAN, *her eyes filling with tears.*

CURTAIN

PROPERTY PLOT

ACT ONE Scene i

Mantelpiece
  Empty teapot
  Cup and saucer
  Tin of buttons
  Packet of cigarettes (full, open)
  Tin of money
  Purse with money (open)
  Matches (pre-set)
  Mirror with postcards stuck round it
Stool D.R.
  Pile of clothes
  Workbasket (with two needles and cotton set in lid) (Set under clothes)
Armchair
  Cushion
  Envelope
  Jim's jacket
U.S. *end of fireplace*
  Jim's shoes
Corner Cupboard
  Book
  Glasses
  Papers
Table C.
  Check tablecloth
  Cut loaf (open)
  Open butter dish
  Three cups, saucers and spoons
  Pile of papers
  Open magazine
Sideboard
  Radio
  Bottle of tomato sauce
  Packet of cornflakes
  Two glasses (pre-set)
  Table mat
  Ashtray
  Family photograph
  Four cups (pre-set)
  Gramophone (lid down, needle on record)
  On it:
    Wooden tray under pile of papers and red sweater

R. *drawer:*
  Two pencils
  Bottle opener
  Small magazine
  Pair of braces
Cutlery tray:
  Four knives
  Three forks
  Three small spoons
  Three large spoons
L. *drawer:*
  White tablecloth (pre-set)
  "Daily Express" (pre-set)
R. *cupboard:*
  Bottle of pale ale (pre-set)
  Three side plates
  Three cereal bowls
  Three cups, three saucers
  Toast rack
  Marmalade jar
  Milk jug
  Sugar basin and spoon (practical)
  Check tablecloth
D.L. *by broken wall*
  Ironing board with pile of clothes on U.S. end and iron on D.S. end with lead
  hanging down (not plugged in)

ACT ONE Scene 2

Flap table
  Bowl of spring flowers
  Airmail envelope with letter
Coffee table
  Tray with two cups, saucers and spoons
  Sugar bowl and spoon
  Cigarette jar with four cigarettes in it
  Matches
Gas stove
  Pot of coffee (practical)

ACT ONE Scene 3

Strike
  All food and breakfast things from table
  Papers from floor
  Workbasket from floor
Set
  Sunday paper on stool

Papers on floor above stool
HILDA's shopping-bag L. of armchair
Workbasket L. of stool
Papers with magazine on top, on chair
Second Scene Drop
Strike
Clothes from stool
Set
Clothes from ironing-board on to table
Plug in iron
Set lid of gramophone up
Tuck chair left of table in
Move ironing-board to R.
Personal

JIM	Packet of cigarettes
BRIAN	Two £1 notes
	Debate notes
AMY	Wedding ring
	Hair pins
GEORGIE	Handbag

Props set offstage for Act One

GEORGIE'S FLAT

In bedroom
JIM's cardigan
On hanger on bedroom door
GEORGIE's négligée

PRESTONS' FLAT

Off in hall
Full milk bottle
JIM's overcoat
Sunday paper
Clothes brush
Pile of records in covers
Tray No. 1
Teapot (practical)
Three glasses of fruit juice
Full milk jug and sugar bowl and spoon
Tray No. 2
Plate of steak, chips and tomatoes
Spoon, knife and fork
Salt, pepper and mustard
Cup for AMY to break
Prop knife with fat on it
Off R. *to be set in Scene Drop*
Hilda's shopping-bag

Sunday paper
Pile of papers

Props set onstage for Act Two

During interval
  Check tea made and set in teapot *Off* in kitchen
Strike
  All untidy dressings
  Tablecloth from C. table and set in cupboard
  Ironing-board and clothes
  Cornflakes from sideboard
Set
  Chair in place of ironing-board
  In cupboard
    Blue book
  On table U.R.
    Pile of textbooks
  Check table C. moved slightly to L.
Set on sideboard
  Morning paper
  Three cereal bowls, three sideplates
  Three cups and saucers
  Salt, pepper and mustard
  Sauce bottle
  Table mat
  Marmalade jar
  Butter dish
  Three fruit-juice glasses
  Milk jug and sugar basin
  Toast rack
  (As much of this as possible on wooden tray on gramophone)
  Family photo turned down
  Check also three cups *on sideboard*
  In R. Drawer
    Check three large spoons, three small spoons, three forks, three knives
First Scene Drop
Strike
  Everything from C. table to kitchen
  Tablecloth to prompt side
Second Scene Drop
Set
  Tablecloth (folded) and pile of papers fixed to fall in second shelf of corner
    cupboard

Props set offstage for Act Two

Off in hall
  JIM's coat

GEORGIE's handbag
Shopping-bag containing half bottle of Red Label Scotch whisky
"New Scientist" in wrapper
Two £1 notes
Debate notes
Off in kitchen
  JIM's shoes
  Teapot (practical)
  Towel
  Tray No. 1
    Tin tray of crockery and cutlery (to be broken)
  Tray No. 2
    Wooden tray with two cups of black coffee (practical)
    Milk jug, sugar basin and spoon, two spoons
  Tray No. 3
    Blue tray with two cups of tea (practical)
    One cup of tea—separate
Off in bedroom
  AMY's dress on hanger
  Small suitcase of clothes
  AMY's dressing-gown and slippers